T0383184

Four-Cornered Leadership

A Framework for Making Decisions

Four-Cornered Leadership

A Framework for Making Decisions

John Roland Schultz

CRC Press
Taylor & Francis Group
Boca Raton London New York

CRC Press is an imprint of the
Taylor & Francis Group, an **informa** business
A PRODUCTIVITY PRESS BOOK

CRC Press
Taylor & Francis Group
6000 Broken Sound Parkway NW, Suite 300
Boca Raton, FL 33487-2742

First issued in hardback 2019

© 2014 by John Roland Schultz
CRC Press is an imprint of Taylor & Francis Group, an Informa business

No claim to original U.S. Government works

ISBN-13: 978-1-4665-9289-6 (hbk)

Library of Congress Cataloging-in-Publication Data

Schultz, John Roland, 1939-
    Four-cornered leadership : a framework for making decisions / John Roland Schultz.
      pages cm
    Includes bibliographical references and index.
    ISBN 978-1-4665-9289-6 (hardback)
    1. Leadership. 2. Decision making. I. Title.

HD57.7.S385 2013
658.4'092--dc23
                                         2013025259

Visit the Taylor & Francis Web site at
http://www.taylorandfrancis.com

and the CRC Press Web site at
http://www.crcpress.com

This book is dedicated to our two boys, sons now grown, who have been challenging but enjoyed and loved, each unique and a leader in his own way: John and Vernon.

Contents

Preface

Is leadership a role or a mind-set? Are there differences that separate leaders from managers? These are questions that frequently arise when people attempt to define leadership. It is a topic that arouses emotions and brings out many competing viewpoints. The opinions offered usually diverge over a continuum, with one end grounded in research and the other in perception.

This book is about leadership. It describes a set of competencies that are based on four core principles that convey very different assumptions about people and organizations. Leadership in this case is about action and the knowledge that is gained when ideas are tested through practice. It is knowing how interdependencies affect the system people work in, knowing how variation—the normal difference between process contingencies—affects system stability and instability, knowing how people learn and develop so organizational capability can be increased, and knowing how individual behaviors can be structured and aligned toward the organization's common good. A distinctive way for viewing leadership is presented, one that is based on learning and continual modification in response to prevailing conditions. Goals are accomplished without force. People are brought onboard in a common effort toward shared sacrifice, struggle, and rewards. Effective leadership is the result of practical application. It is recognized and honored after the fact because events have demonstrated an ability to bring about meaningful change.

Leadership is a theme that receives considerable attention. Certainly, there is a large amount of material devoted to the subject. Libraries catalog and shelve numerous titles about the topic. Anyone interested in becoming a leader can—through effort—promote themselves by applying what is already known. Leaders, nevertheless, come and go. Some are successful for a while and then flame out as the enterprises they lead come crashing down. Recent circumstances have produced many failures in finance, industry, and politics. The consequences have been economically devastating, with failures in every sector. The individuals society has looked to for leadership have not facilitated improvement—have not delivered.

Often, people are called leaders because of the position they hold. However, leadership is dependent on situational circumstances and the needs of those who are disposed to follow. Leaders can arise at any time and are found at all organizational levels. Leadership is really a skill set that can be learned and applied by anyone. Persona and individual appearance—traits and personal characteristics—are not as important as the ability to cope with and manage situational demands. The concepts described in this book are process oriented, are adaptable under varying conditions, and are oriented around the four elements that comprise the system of profound knowledge. This leadership philosophy was first proposed by W. Edwards Deming, and places emphasis on the physical and tangible elements in a workplace that can be studied, analyzed, and modified to create a more productive yet enjoyable environment. Leadership in this setting is about moving ahead and getting work done without violating commonly held values or manipulating and forcing people to do what is not in their own best interests.

Leaders are successful because they are able to rally others to a cause—to a purpose—with events creating benefits for everyone involved. So, leadership is not about tough-mindedness or incentives, using the right combination of rewards and reprimand, particularly for those who choose to follow. These are people who willingly subordinate a portion of their individuality to achieve results that the leader has deemed important. Simply put, the leader with the help of others brings about change. Leadership does not exist without delighted followers and a common vision realized through cooperative purposeful action. Leadership is tested and judged by the results that are produced.

Each of the four elements comprising the system of profound knowledge is analyzed and examined in relation to prevailing management and organizational theory. These concepts are not new, but ordered and presented as a tangible foundation for internalizing Deming's philosophy as a practical leadership method. The connection between the four elements and an individual's ability to lead is defined by proficiencies that are learnable and transferable to any organizational setting in government, industry, or education. Dispelled are popular notions about leadership characteristics, such as good looks, determination, persuasiveness, eloquence, forcefulness, decisiveness, and bottom-line thinking.

Although there is plenty of material dedicated to leadership and management theory, none of it has comprehensively explored the system of profound knowledge as a leadership tool—a method for getting work done that is based on understanding organizational complexity and follower needs. The intended audience for this book is newly appointed leaders, managers, and supervisors who have excellent technical skills but have not been exposed to the proficiencies or emotional concepts that typify a capable and effective leader. In addition, any person in a position of authority who is trying to adopt the principles of quality management and continuous improvement will find this book helpful and empowering.

Four-Cornered Leadership is the perfect guide for individuals who feel leadership is about building follower capabilities—being an inspirational coach and mentor focused on long-term gain that is the result of continual learning and renewal. The content is down to earth, easy to understand, and clearly written. The information is presented in bite-size and meaningful chunks supported by charts and graphs. The content arrangement and bulleted points are designed to appeal to the visual learner.

The five chapters that directly support the system of profound knowledge are Chapter 2, "Understand the Importance of System Interdependencies"; Chapter 3, "Understand Why People Behave as They Do"; Chapter 4, "Understand How People Learn, Develop, and Improve"; Chapter 5, "Understand the Variability of Work"; and Chapter 7, "Manage Interaction Dynamics." These relationships are illustrated by Figure P.1.

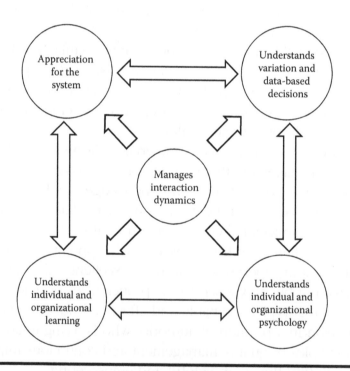

Figure P.1 The system of profound knowledge.

About the Author

John Roland Schultz is an independent management consultant and retired college professor. For 20 years, he taught management and supervisory development courses and was a program director overseeing an advanced technical certificate in quality management. Prior to teaching, his work experience included 25 years as a consultant, technical services manager, and new product development engineer. He has performed doctoral study in adult education, has a master of science degree in management, and has undergraduate degrees with a focus on industrial management and organizational behavior.

Chapter 1

Leadership Defined

The job of management is not supervision, but leadership. ... The aim of leadership should be to improve the performance of man and machine, to improve quality, to increase output, and to simultaneously bring pride of workmanship to people.

Deming, 1986, p. 54

Often, people think leadership, even from Deming's viewpoint, is the result of specific traits or persona that if possessed predestine an individual to a position of prominence. Still others feel it is all about tough-mindedness—the ability to gain control through force of will. But, neither is true, and this verdict is supported by years of scholarly research. Leaders can be found at all organizational levels and are able to rally people to a cause because their skills and abilities match a particular set of follower needs and situational circumstances. These are competencies that can be learned and practiced by anyone with the motivation to step forward.

This chapter helps characterize Four-Cornered Leadership as realized through W. Edwards Deming's system of profound knowledge and sets the stage for its application. The following topics define current thinking about leadership and present several examples:

- Leadership and profound knowledge
- Leadership competencies
- Leadership, power, and followers
- Leadership and management
- Leadership approaches
- Leadership implications

Leadership and Profound Knowledge

Many individuals have a grandiose vision of leadership. This image may have more to do with the pretentious behavior displayed sometimes by visible and important people. Most may think this style of governance has always existed, but it has not, and change is seriously needed. The system of profound knowledge that will unfold in the following chapters is a way to alter current thinking. The following story about a spellbinding personality demonstrates this present-day and popular point of view:

> Gertrud Grossmund was the president of a historically acclaimed college. She was well spoken and recognized by the community at large as a forward-thinking individual who had introduced strategic planning and consensus management at the college. To the faculty and staff, however, she was viewed as a rather flamboyant self-promoter and a wheeler-dealer who was a masterful talker. Articulate and savvy, she was able to present a convincing image. For example, when board positions opened for appointment, she used her reputation and influence in the community to seat people who, captivated by her self-assurance and persuasive manner, were affable to her many and far-reaching ideas.
>
> Upon arriving five years ago, she set about replacing the executive-level deans with new executive-level vice presidents. The realigned positions included those in financial

services, administrative services, student services, instructional services, information services and human resources. All the new arrivals were capable individuals who were friendly and generally well liked by their staff. Yet, each was no match in stature, eloquence, or demeanor to Grossmund. These people were diligent but unusually quiet and unassuming. They acted at Grossmund's behest but never stepped forward with their own ideas. She seemed to have had a knack for picking introverts who went out of their way to avoid controversy.

Grossmund would hold a monthly open meeting—she called them forums—with students. When confronted with difficult issues, she would wholeheartedly agree but then counter with a plausible explanation. Speaking brilliantly and in a measured directive tone, she would offer a solution that the crowd found appealing and compelling. Many nodded their heads in agreement, yet when all was said and done, students left questioning the exact sequence of reasoning and the logic that had won them over. This ability to sell ideas and convince others to follow was used on staff and faculty alike. In the end, however, individuals often wondered to what they had agreed.

Of course, as time went on, people began to realize that many issues were left to fester, and that grand ideas never came to realization. Although there were yearly reorganizations, with departments shuffled and reshuffled and deans or department chairs promoted or reassigned, opportunities were missed, and enrollments did not grow in proportion to other schools within the state system. In the end, after one sabbatical too many, pressure from the community, and a loss-of-confidence declaration by faculty, the board asked for Grossmund's resignation.

Real leaders create opportunities and value people primarily for their talent and ability to contribute. They invite people to meetings to look for ideas and find solutions but do not dominate the discussion. They facilitate by asking the right questions. Real leaders are not afraid to advance subordinates' ideas and make a case for their realization. Yet, people are drawn to individuals who appear strong, deliberate, and willing to take control. Why are style and flair such compelling lures?

We live in a complex world where many institutions are having difficulty sustaining a meaningful and coherent existence over an extended period. Some organizations seem to function well for a while, but then falter as competitive and economic pressures expose vulnerabilities. News stories document the many failures of business and government. Some individuals feel organizations have become too large, and that leaders are not in touch with public needs. Disgruntled interest groups demand results, while the disenfranchised raise questions about fair and ethical conduct and wonder what can be done. They cling to the hope that big ideas accompanied by swagger and bravado will get them to a "promised land."

Leadership is a topic that has received considerable attention. Libraries catalog and shelve numerous titles devoted to its practice. Similarly, leadership has a variety of meanings. The following definitions are just a few examples:

- "There are no bad soldiers under a good general" (Siu, 1980, p. 303).
- "Leadership is the pivotal force behind successful organizations, and to create vital viable organizations, leadership is necessary to develop a new vision of what the organization can be, and then mobilize the organization's ability to change toward the new vision" (Bennis and Nanus, 1985, p. 2).
- "Leading is the central part of a manager's role, which involves working with and through others to achieve organizational goals" (Stoner and Freeman, 1989, p. 459).
- "The job of a leader is to accomplish the transformation of his organization. He possesses knowledge, personality, and persuasive power" (Deming, 1994, p. 116).
- "Leadership defines what the future should look like, aligns people with that vision, and inspires them to make it happen despite the obstacles" (Kotter, 1996, p. 25).
- "Leadership is the presence and spirit of the individual who leads and the relationship created with those who are led" (Scholtes, 1998, p. 372).

What are the conclusions that can be drawn about leadership after considering these statements? For most current thinkers, there are several assumptions. First, leaders create meaningful results. Second, they do not do it by themselves. And third, they have a future perspective that enables them to establish a sense of ongoing direction. Leaders, through training, experience, or personal aptitude, are able to convince others to achieve results that are deemed desirable by both leader and followers. Working together, they are able to alter common circumstances and achieve advantageous results.

For centuries, leaders have been rallying people to greater accomplishment: to win wars, build empires, and of course complete the mundane rigors of day-to-day work. It seems the world has been able to produce leaders sufficient to match almost every challenge. Certainly, there has been enough written on the topic. Anyone interested in becoming a leader can—through effort—promote herself or himself by applying what is already known. Then, why is a new system of leadership needed?

This new system is needed because—as many now realize—recent circumstances have produced too many failures in finance, industry, and politics. The consequences have been economically devastating, with losses in every sector: numerous bank closures, a construction industry in collapse, an auto industry struggling to recover, jobs and whole industrial segments leaving the country, and an economy in deep recession. The individuals who society has looked to for leadership have not facilitated improvement or a better society. Stewardship responsible for this tragedy has been close to criminal, with bottom-line schemes that focused on short-term gain and self-serving pocket-stuffing behavior.

Well, something can be done; however, it will take leadership—not the traditional kind, but profound leadership, a different leadership, one that is transformational and has at its core a set of principles that produces benefit for all stakeholders, not just a privileged few. Deming's system of profound knowledge provides a different viewpoint on leadership. Its ideas and underlying principles were first shaped by the 1980s' economic downturn, a period when the quality of U.S. products reached rock bottom, and the demand for foreign goods steadily increased while domestic manufacturing slowly declined. This was the first of many subsequent crises—boom-and-bust cycles—for which business and political leadership ignored the lessons and costs of past mistakes.

The system of profound knowledge is a theory of related principles that requires a leader, or manager for that matter, to consider all organizational aspects when making decisions. This means recognizing how processes are interconnected and how they function as a whole within the larger environment so that the organization can reach intended expectations. This system of leadership has at its foundation the following four parts:

- *Appreciation for the system:* This appreciation is the ability to understand the relationship between system components—suppliers, producers, and customers—and how they contribute toward the overall good of the organization, its stakeholders, and adjoining environment.
- *Knowledge about variation:* This knowledge is about the ability to recognize that two data points do not make a trend, and that all systems vary over time, sometimes positively and sometimes negatively; however, the information produced can provide guidance about what is normal and what is abnormal and indicate when to take action.
- *Theory of knowledge:* This is the ability to understand how people learn and how to advance their ability to make decisions, improve the work process, and contribute to the organization's common good.
- *Knowledge of psychology:* This knowledge provides the ability to recognize why people behave as they do, then create an environment—not one based on slogans, quotes, incentives, or exhortations—in which individual differences and skills are used to optimize the system for everyone's benefit.

Each of the components is analyzed and discussed in further chapters. However, as a catalyst for leadership, they cannot be separated and applied individually. All elements interact with one another to create a comprehensive strategy for leading others and managing individual behavior. Deming (1994), in his book *The New Economics*, framed the benefits this way:

> Once the individual understands the system of profound knowledge, he will apply its principles to every kind of relationship with other people. He will have a basis for judgment of his own decisions and for the transformation of the organization that he belongs to. The individual, once transformed, will:
>
> ■ Set an example
> ■ Be a good listener, but will not compromise
> ■ Continually teach other people
> ■ Help people to pull away from their current practice and beliefs and move into the new philosophy without feeling guilty about the past. (p. 93)

As a side note, although Deming often uses the pronoun *he*, leadership is gender neutral. Leaders can come from any walk of life and often step up under what some would consider humdrum conditions. However, it is the results of an individual's stewardship that determine his or her stature and ability as a leader.

Leadership Competencies

Leadership is a topic many people have difficulty defining. There are multiple and varying points of view. Some focus on the ability to create wealth, while others consider the managerial aspects of planning, organizing, directing, and controlling. Still others look for traits and behaviors like charisma that set leaders apart from the rest of the managerial crowd. Regardless of how leadership is defined, there are interpersonal influences that encourage people to subordinate as followers. In general terms, successful leaders exhibit the following characteristics:

■ *Influence:* Leaders are able to fashion a vision that has current and future relevance, then communicate the vision in terms that others readily accept as their own. People look to the leader for direction that will guide their effort toward a better future.

■ *Know-How:* Leaders are able to comprehend circumstantial factors and then create enabling processes and structures that will allow others to accomplish the vision. The leader has the right knowledge and appropriate skills to get people through a particular situation or to a desired result.

■ *Standing:* Leaders are able to place themselves in a position so others are willing to trust and accept direction that will harmonize collective efforts for followers to accomplish the vision. Either by personal choice or by communal vote, people allow the leader to channel and direct their activities.

Individuals who display these capabilities have developed a set of skills that provisions them to command in a leadership position. The system of profound knowledge has, at its core, competencies that support the three leadership characteristics. The skills that typify a capable and profoundly effective leader are the following:

■ *Articulates a compelling future:* The leader is able to define and communicate the organization's principal purpose.
■ *Focuses on the long term:* The leader is able to create a map that focuses attention on the organization's long-term

survival. Short-term objectives do not become distractions that restrict continual assessment and ongoing improvement.

- *Centers diverse efforts so the whole system benefits:* The leader is able to manage the organization as a system by eliminating barriers between component parts so people can work together as a team for the common good.
- *Provides for enabling structures:* The leader is able to facilitate the development of an infrastructure that accommodates the diverse nature of human behavior and coordinates individual activities so actions align with both long-term goals and short-term objectives.
- *Appreciates the impact of variation:* The leader is able to recognize the inherent variability of organizational influences and individual activities, distinguish what is normal, and understand the kind of action to take in response to different conditions. The corresponding reply is based on data gathered over time and not point-to-point comparisons.
- *Facilitates individual and organizational development:* The leader is able to provide for the development of individual and organizational capabilities by increasing access to information and learning so people working together can solve problems, make decisions, and contribute to the organization's or group's well-being.
- *Arouses behaviors and actions that contribute to the common good:* The leader understands human behavior and uses positive reinforcement and intrinsic motivators to inspire actions that achieve outcomes aligned with the group's needs and organization's overall purpose.
- *Displays personal credibility:* The leader is able to establish a sense of personal credibility that sets an example by displaying personal ethics, managing emotions, and taking responsibility for the results of individual and subordinate actions.

Leadership competencies are the defining skills that drive the system of profound knowledge and thus the expression of leadership characteristics. The leader's power—ability to exert influence, channel individual behaviors, and actions—is contingent on this distinct set of skills and their able execution. Although many feel that leaders possess unique traits or present a particular persona, research indicates otherwise. Leadership consists of nothing more than a set of competencies that can be learned and practiced by most people. The ability to apply these skills is of course dependent on situational and emotional factors—the group's needs and circumstances and the individual leader's capability and good judgment. In any case, leadership is an important aspect in organizational success or failure and can be found in formal and informal settings and at all organizational levels.

Leadership, Power, and Followers

Leadership, although subject to a certain amount of give-and-take collaboration, involves an unequal distribution of power. The leader is in a position where others subordinate their actions based on the leader's desires. Having control over someone else's behavior is power. Power is the ability to make things happen in a particular way.

Leaders do have power, and that influence can be derived in several ways—either through individual acumen or because of situational factors. However, there are limits to how people will respond to or be influenced by the use of power. A business or organization, for example, may flourish for many years while under a particular leader's direction, but as conditions or relationships change, the enterprise begins to struggle and ultimately lose market share. Unhappy investors press for a better return, and the board of directors responds. Later, after a new leader replaces the old one, the organization once again becomes vital and energetic. So, power has contingencies that are based on behavioral dynamics and environmental conditions.

Power can be derived from two sources: organizational and individual. These motives were first described by French and Raven (1962). Organizational power is based on the leader's formal authority or position in the hierarchy. Individual power is based on personal intelligence and the popular sentiment of followers. Table 1.1 summarizes these aspects of power. Power implies the person in a leadership position has extraordinary control over follower actions and behavior, that through brute force—the manipulation of information, resources, and reprimand—a desired response can be attained. This notion assumes that followers have no choice in the matter or lack self-determination. In some cases, this may be true, but in most organizational and sociopolitical settings, people have options. They can quit, go on strike, reduce their output, protest and sabotage leader directives, or engage in a campaign to overthrow the status quo and gain control.

So, being in a position of authority does not have guarantees and may in fact have implicit and explicit obligations based on tradition or legal and ethical principles. However, there does appear to be a rather large zone of indifference for followers. This refers to the degree of obedience or tendency to follow directives even if outcome may be questionable. That is why influential people often get their way and typically do so for extended periods.

Stanley Milgram (1964) of Yale University designed an experiment to test the limits of influence when people were given orders by an authority figure, even if the result appeared to injure another individual. Subjects were asked to administer electric shocks to increase someone else's learning ability at the behest and continued urging of an overly directive trainer. The results were surprising and indicated that people have the tendency to accept and comply with demands even under dubious circumstances. Roughly 65 percent of the subjects continued to shock learners even when these individuals appeared to be in great pain. Only 35 percent refused to obey the experimenter at some lower overriding moment.

Table 1.1 Sources of Power

Organizational	
Legitimate power	This form of influence is based on a person's formal authority or lawful right to occupy a particular spot in an organization's hierarchy. Usually, an individual in this position has been elected or appointed and is entitled to manage and direct the activities of those within an assigned sphere of control.
Reward power	This form of influence is based on a person's ability to use extrinsic and intrinsic rewards to control the behavior and output of others. For example, influence in the form of compliments, improved working conditions, promotions, or money is used to induce desirable actions.
Oppressive power	This form of influence is based on a person's ability to intimidate. It is the opposite side of reward power and uses punishment as a means of control. Typically, resources and privileges are removed, and individuals are subjected to increasing demands and criticism.
Individual	
Expert power	This form of influence is based on a person's knowledge, experience, or good judgment. Others are willing to accept direction and advice because they recognize the leader's expertise works to their advantage. For example, a physician or consultant has expert power. A manufacturing engineer may make recommendations on how to lower production costs and improve operating efficiencies based on expert power.
Referent power	This form of influence is based on a person's popularity, demeanor, ability to perform, or position in the hierarchy. Others are willing to accommodate the leader because they have a personal affinity or fondness for the individual in charge. In essence, subordinates admire and identify with the leader and derive a certain amount of prestige from the association and will act to preserve the relationship.

Why did this happen, and what are the implications for those in a leadership position? First, through training and experience, people are taught to respect and admire authority. Business leaders, politicians, entertainers, teachers, and the wealthy are typically looked up to and admired. Second, there is an implied social contract between individuals and their institutions. It defines the relationship in terms of rights, privileges, and obligations in a manner that tends to favor organizational authority. People are conditioned to respond deferentially to those in control. They have been socialized to accept orders from persons of a higher status or institutional position.

But, there are limits to the zone of indifference, and what is tolerable and acceptable can change as circumstances change. Take for example, the position of secretarial assistant. At one time, making the office coffee, shopping for the boss during lunch hour, or typing papers for the boss's children were just part of the job and within the zone of indifference. However, today these activities are beyond responsibility because job expectations have changed. In addition, continual demands or exhortations for better quality, service, or productivity that are not accompanied by enabling structures or resources will ultimately fall outside the zone of indifference and be rejected and challenged. Being in a position of authority, in the end, means the leader has to lead and do so with more than bluster, good looks, or fancy talk.

People will follow an authority figure, but that person has to be perceived as legitimate. Certain conditions exist where organizational group members can agree that the basis for the implied contract that governs their behavior is worthwhile and provides mutual benefits. For example, a company president, or supervisor in many cases, will be obeyed if there is consensus among followers about fairness of the system that appointed the leader and the rules that govern the working relationship. A manager's orders will be accepted and most likely followed when these subsequent conditions are met:

- The directive or order is unquestionably understood.
- The directive or order is perceived as in the group's or organization's best interest.
- The directive or order is believed to be consistent with prevailing values.
- The subordinate or group has the capability and wherewithal to carry out the directive or order.

Most people will seek a balance between what they will do or contribute and what is gained in return. The relationship between leader and follower is one of deference, but only by consent.

Leadership and Management

There are distinctions between leadership and management. Each position has its own characteristics and functional activities, but these activities are related and complementary arrangements for coordinating and controlling organizational operations. Leaders typically operate at the top of a hierarchy and managers at lower levels. But, that does not mean that managers are not capable leaders. In many cases, managers have to be leaders as well as coordinators and controllers of complex transactions.

Management is an organizational construct. It exists because large public and private-sector enterprises would find their existence—because of the many inputs and multifaceted process interactions—difficult, if not impossible, without such oversight. Accordingly, management is all about dealing with complex operations. These are practices and procedures concerned with planning, organizing, staffing, controlling, and then problem solving so activities function at some kind of optimal level. Management is concerned with the immediate and day-to-day activities, and making sure organizational transactions are completed efficiently and effectively.

Leadership, on the other hand, is about the long term, staying relevant, and coping with changing economic and sociopolitical forces. These include competition, unstable markets, money to finance short-term obligations, overcapacity, an inefficient supply chain, an underperforming workforce, and the constant pressure by stockholders for higher and higher returns. Consequently, what works today will not necessarily work tomorrow. The need to adapt and change becomes a necessity for survival and growth. Leadership at its core is about coping with the need for constant improvement.

John Kotter (1990) suggests the difference between management and leadership is defined by specific but balancing activities. The symbiotic nature of this relationship, an adaptation of his thinking, is summarized by contrasting the leadership process with the management process of planning, organizing, and controlling.

> ***Setting direction versus planning and budgeting:*** The leader develops a future purpose and the accompanying strategies that will facilitate change toward the vision. Managers set the intervening targets and goals, establish and sequence the action steps, and allocate resources so that plans and, in due course the organization's overall purpose, are achieved.
>
> ***Aligning people versus organizing and staffing:*** The leader brings people together—workers and stakeholders—in a common and committed effort that is aimed at achieving the organization's purpose or vision. This means communicating the intended purpose and direction so that others understand what needs to be done and remain committed to its achievement. Managers, on the other hand, create organizational structures capable of accomplishing plan requirements, staff the appropriate jobs with qualified people, and assign sufficient authority and responsibility to ensure implementation is achieved.

Inspiring people versus controlling and problem solving: The leader keeps people moving in the right direction, despite obstacles and challenges, by appealing to basic human needs, values, and emotions. In this case, the leader needs to set an example—walk the talk—and create an atmosphere where people can participate by taking control of their own destiny. Managers, conversely, need to empower others and create an environment where the workforce is willing to take risks and make decisions. In addition, managers must create control mechanisms that can monitor results and signal when corrective action and problem solving are needed so effort remains focused on short-term results and the long-term vision.

Yes, managers and leaders do have different responsibilities, but their roles are not exclusive. They are joined in a mutual and beneficial relationship where leaders champion possibilities and managers subdue complexities. This, however, does not mean that managers and supervisors are not sufficiently expert to be leaders. Quite the opposite, these individuals are leaders at their own level and should be able to act with the same profound knowledge that an effective chief executive has.

Leadership Approaches

There are three major approaches to leadership. Two have classic relevance and are considered by many as a way to achieve dominance at the top of an organization or political institution. The first is concerned with traits—physical and personal characteristics that make someone stand apart in the pecking order. The second approach attempts to identify emotional behaviors that might signify leadership capability. Both these approaches assume that persona and the way a person behaves are more important than intervening situational or environmental factors, and that good looks, demeanor, and mental deftness trump a cascade of situational demands.

But, research and current thinking have fashioned a third approach that considers organizational influences, follower needs, and the leader's ability to respond as conditions change. It is commonly identified as the contingency approach. This view recognizes that leader effectiveness is variable and, to a great extent, tested and battered by ever-changing external forces. The leadership method that arises from this perspective is based on eventualities and the leader using a behavioral style that is appropriate to a large number of causal variables.

> ***The trait approach to leadership:*** One of the first methods for studying leadership concentrated on character traits. The idea of trying to identify qualities that defined a great person dates back more than century. Inherent personal characteristics like appearance (physique, height, and weight); intelligence; ability to speak; and dominance were thought to be significant indicators. Obviously, not all individuals had these traits, so only those who did were presumed to be effective leaders. This line of thinking, nevertheless, ignored the impact of training and experience on potential ability. It implied leadership is an inborn quality, and that leaders can be screened from nonleaders by simply observing for character traits.
>
> Over time, however, attempts to compare the characteristics of effective against ineffective leaders began to show flaws. Traits alone could not explain why some leaders were successful in one set of circumstances and not in another. Studies began to suggest that leadership is a complex and dynamic process that is impacted by other variables, such as the leader's behavior, follower expectations, and organizational complexities. It became clear that a stately appearance, a commanding voice, and

a clever mind were not accurate predictors of competent leadership. Often, those individuals with the classic and characteristic leadership persona failed to deliver under changing and diverse conditions. Another set of criteria was needed to assess leader fitness.

The behavioral approach to leadership: When it became apparent that a particular set of physiological characteristics did not define an effective leader, researchers began to look at behavioral attributes. These included such things as knowledge, initiative, ability to delegate, ability to motivate, self-confidence, and many more. But, unlike hypothetical inborn traits, behaviors can be learned and therefore transferred to others. If the right set of behaviors could be identified, it was thought, effective leaders could be trained.

Nevertheless, a definitive list of behaviors was difficult to pin down. Similar to traits, behaviors that worked in one place often failed in others. As an example, someone who was technically skilled but slightly introverted and functioning well in a manufacturing setting often faltered when moved to an organization like a consumer products company that required a more extroverted and marketing-savvy style. Ultimately, it became apparent that effective behavior needed to match an organization's culture and the demands of its particular environment.

A number of studies looked at leadership behaviors in terms of function. Researchers began to consider the context and tasks performed in various situations. The results produced two types of leader behavior—those that were employee centered and those that were work centered. Depending on the research group, these complementary leader behaviors were given different labels and depicted as a range of styles along a continuum or as a pattern of styles described by a two-axis grid. One axis was attentiveness to relationship building, and the other axis was attentiveness to task accomplishment.

Theorists first described leadership as an array of behaviors along a scale that went from being boss centered to employee centered. These researchers tended to favor more democratic styles. But, acknowledged leaders and managers needed to select a style of behavior that matched prevailing conditions. Leadership in this case was defined by a singular temperament based on the amount of authority used in relation to the amount of freedom allowed for subordinates. On the other hand, the research groups that used a grid approach understood that leader behavior or style was probably multidimensional. For example, a leader might be concerned about worker relationships and their impact on production but also had to decide how and when the work got done. Leaders often displayed behaviors that were employee centered as well as task centered, not just one or the other.

The contingency approach to leadership: This perspective on leadership recognizes that traits and behaviors are subject to organizational events—that the leader's response must be appropriate to situational factors to achieve desired outcomes. Contingency approaches tried to identify particular circumstances and then prescribe a leadership style that would work in a particular situation.

Fred Fiedler (Fiedler, Chemers, and Mahar, 1976) suggests there are three situational factors that determine which leadership approach will be effective:

■ *Leader–member relationship:* This describes the extent to which members and the leader get along. A strong working relationship is one shaped by mutual respect. Formal rank or authority is not the reason group members accept the leader's influence. On the other hand, a weak relationship is one built on leader control and low regard for member concerns.

- *Task structure:* Task structure depicts the extent of clarity in work structures as opposed to disarray and uncertainty. Structured situations have clear goals and well-defined methods; unstructured situations have ambiguous goals and muddled routines.
- *Power position:* This factor defines the position a leader holds in the chain of command. The president of an organization has more power than the manager of engineering. However, others may compete for status because of know-how, trust, or admiration. The leader possesses both organizational and personal power.

Fiedler et al. (1976) also suggest there are two leadership approaches that can be applied, but each is situationally effective:

- *Task-motivated approach:* The leader focuses on getting the job done. The reaction of work groups and managers is less important than maintaining goals and reaching objectives.
- *Relationship-motivated approach:* The leader is able to build warm personal relationships with coworkers and regards close ties with managers as important to overall success.

Confronted by changeable contingencies, effective leadership should vary tactics according to the situation. Table 1.2 illustrates which approach to use based on situational factors. The conditional dynamics affecting individuals in a leadership position are as follows:

1. When conditions are favorable—people are in tune with the leader and work is getting accomplished—the approach should be group decision making and goal setting with an ongoing focus on direction. Be willing to delegate responsibility and authority.

Table 1.2 Situational Factors and Leadership Approach

	Situational Conditions		
Situational Factors	*Favorable*	*Confused*	*Unfavorable*
Relationship	Good	Mixed: Some good, others poor	Poor
Task structure	Structured	Muddled: Some structured, others unstructured	Unstructured
Power position	Strong	Mixed: Some strong, others weak	Weak
Leadership approach	Task oriented and low control	Relationship oriented	Task oriented and high control

2. When conditions are confused—some people are with the leader, and others are still not committed—the approach should strengthen and build relationships. Use give-and-take communication and group participation to establish methods, provide ongoing feedback, and reinforce the focus on objectives.

3. When conditions are unfavorable—relations are poor, and the leader's position is weak—the approach should provide for considerable work group support and a continued emphasis on direction. Focus on goals and outcomes, be specific about expectations and measures for results, solicit and share information, and promote the benefits of the new approach.

Although there is recognition that leadership behaviors vary and the projected style should probably match follower needs and situational conditions, many researchers, particularly Feidler, felt it was difficult for individuals to adapt and alter their innate behaviors. Personality and distinguishing conduct are the result of early life influence and the way individuals are socialized. The style that is developed and adopted is fixed by intrinsic processes and probably not flexible. It would be better, therefore, for a prospective leader to understand his or her dominant style and chose the right situation. As a case in point, Grossmund, the flamboyant and persuasive leader described previously in this chapter, was successful for a number of years. Her style tended to be authoritarian but was concerned with managing relationships. This complex combination of personality characteristics helped her survive under a particular set of conditions. However, as circumstances matured and changed, her limits for adaptability were reached. In the end, after resigning, she moved on to another college, one that was newly chartered, where her personal need for control and authority will work well for a while. Task orientation and masterful control, accompanied by the ability to build relationships, succeed in conditions where there is uncertainty and untested structures. But, as conditions settle and stabilize, her inherent need to be in control will be at odds with other people's need for collegiality—the sharing of power.

The situational leadership model developed by Paul Hersey and Kenneth Blanchard (1982) also recognizes a multidimensional leadership style—behaviors that are a combination of relationship orientation and task orientation—in response to follower maturity. Follower maturity is described as a continuum from immature to mature and includes the following four stages:

- *Low maturity:* People are unwilling and unable, or lack the confidence, to take responsibility and get something done. Their actions do not meet task expectations. The work group requires considerable direction, reassurance, and remedial development through training.
- *Moderate maturity:* People are willing and confident but unable to take meaningful responsibility. Their actions are lackluster because skills are not sufficient for the task at hand. Those in the work group merit less support and

reinforcement because of their willingness but require significant direction and training to compensate for the lack of skills.

- *Moderately high maturity:* People at this level of maturity are competent but lack confidence and a sense of security. Their actions are deliberate, halting, and painfully slow. The work group requires support, reassurance, and some leader participation through coaching and mentoring.
- *High maturity:* People are both competent and willing to take responsibility for actions that will achieve organizational goals. Their actions are timely and effective. The work group requires little direction and responds well when responsibility and authority are handed over.

Table 1.3 describes appropriate leadership styles for various maturity levels. Suggested are leadership styles that can be effective at helping followers achieve expectations and work toward organizational plans and goals. Contingency approaches to leadership appear to have lessons that are more applicable to managers. However, anyone in a command position can benefit from the findings because leaders often adapt a style or mode of operating that is inflexible and remains constant regardless of conditions. The key conclusion that can be drawn is as follows: Effective leader behavior needs to be adaptive. The leader's response must continually accommodate follower expectations and situation particulars to be effective.

Leadership Implications

What does all of this mean? What are the lessons that can be learned or conclusions that can be drawn? First, leadership is not an inherent intuitive quality that some individuals have and others do not. Second, the leader's job is complex, but the ideas that define and shape the leadership function can be identified and consequently incorporated as one's own.

Table 1.3   Appropriate Leadership Style and Follower Maturity

Follower Maturity	Appropriate Style
Low follower maturity: There is a lack of skills and a low level of ambition.	**High task and low relationship behaviors:** Leader is highly directive, initiates training, and unconditionally explains what needs to be done.
Low-to-moderate follower maturity: There is a high level of confidence but a low level of ability.	**High task and high relationship behaviors:** Leader is somewhat directive but also supportive by providing enabling structures, bringing together diverse or competing efforts, and ensuring ongoing training.
Moderate-to-high level of follower maturity: There is a lack of confidence or willingness but a high level of ability.	**High relationship and low task behaviors:** The leader is focused on building relationships between work groups and ensuring a high level of participation. There is less direction or direct intervention.
High follower maturity: There is a high level of confidence accompanied by a high level of ability.	**Low relationship and low task behaviors:** The leader lets events unfold and has confidence in followers' ability to initiate and carry out work related tasks. There is a high level of delegation and minimal interference.

- Leadership is competency based. The skills can be taught and learned.
- Leadership is like any other ability. Proficiency is gained through coaching by teachers and mentors and through experience in a variety of work settings.
- Leadership behaviors must be adaptive, flexible, and proficient enough to meet the situational needs of followers.
- Leadership can be found at every organizational level. The role can be formal (officially selected) or informal (follower appointed).
- Anyone with sufficient ambition, mental discipline, and emotional maturity has the potential to become a leader.

▪ Leadership based on the principles and competencies found in the system of profound knowledge is transformative and will make any organization more competitive and a place where people are proud to work.

Successful organizations have one major element that sets them apart from those that are unsuccessful. They have leadership that is forward looking, adaptive to changing conditions, and concerned with the cultural processes that make it possible for the workforce to meet organizational goals and expectations. The system of profound knowledge contains these transformative principles that, when applied to leadership, provide a basis for solid judgment and decision making. The remaining chapters examine the system of profound knowledge, its four related parts, and how the elements work together to create a leadership style that is thoughtful, data oriented, reflective, and adaptive.

As a final story, here is a managerial style that exemplifies the Four-Cornered approach to leadership. In a matter-of-fact and nonflamboyant manner, this individual was able to create conditions for meaningful change.

> Bernard Demut was a programmer and project leader with the information technology (IT) department of a large university. He was assigned to work with the university's teaching hospital on an undertaking that would upgrade the billing system. Although the process was automated, there were many complaints by patients of inaccuracies and multiple billing statements. Some were received months after a doctor's visit or procedure.
>
> Demut started by trying to understand the true nature of the problem. He and his small project team surveyed patients and interviewed administrative staff and medical staff. They held meetings with both billing personnel and medical staff where problems were discussed and ideas solicited. Agendas were sent in advance so participants could arrive prepared. The meetings were managed and

facilitated so discussion was open and forthcoming but not dominated by any single individual or small group. The focus was on information gathering and problem solving. Leaps to conclusions and bold statements about how the job should be done were discouraged.

Ultimately, a problem-solving team was formed that included Demut and his group plus representatives from billing, medical staff, and hospital administration. They started by analyzing the previously gathered data and information. The cause appeared to be how information was entered into medical records and also the billing system. Medical records were a mass of pen-on-paper forms and documents. Information had to be recorded twice—coded and reentered into the automated system that supported billing and insurance claims. Hospital administration, primarily the medical director, felt the problem rested with personnel. People charged with recording information were dropping the ball. On the other hand, the team felt the processes of record keeping and billing were the problem—a system problem. They felt a single-entry automated records system was a better solution. But, at that time there was no off-the-shelf system in existence. It would have to be designed by the IT staff.

Demut and the team set about selling their solution to the hospital administration and its medical director. However, they were met with objections about cost and the overwhelming job of converting current paper records into a digital format. Those in charge felt that training was the answer. People just needed to understand how to do their job better. The proposed solution, of course, was eventually shelved. Undeterred, however, Demut and two team members got down to the task of developing an automated patient records system on their own time. Within a year, the partners formed their own company and shortly thereafter approached the hospital and two other hospitals in the community with proposals for an automated and integrated record-keeping system.

Demut, a person who is admittedly introverted and tends to be low key, displays leadership characteristics that will bring about real change—moving people toward a better condition. He is self-confident and is willing to sacrifice time and energy to achieve objectives. His decision making values the information that data and discovery bring. He respects other people's positions and is willing to listen. Meetings are productive occasions where an open exchange of information occurs. He purposely intervenes to manage and balance the discussion. In dealing with people, he prods them to imagine other possibilities and looks at problems from several angles. He is able to interact with people at all levels of the organization and is not overly concerned with his own image or status. Demut demonstrates many of the leadership characteristics that are currently displayed by owners and managers of successful technical startups. These are enjoyable and exciting places to work, where there is a strategic focus, customers are important, and there is balance, openness, and sharing of tasks as well as rewards. Leaders are people who think change is needed and are able to gather others in an effort to create a new reality.

Chapter 2

Chapter 2

Understand the Importance of System Interdependencies

Introduction

Leadership is practiced and deployed within the framework of an organizational structure. This could be an institution such as a business, a healthcare clinic, or a government agency. It might be a functional group such as the military, a labor union, or a political party. An organization is a group of individuals working together in an effort to achieve a particular purpose. Leadership directs the planning, organizing, and controlling of resources, both material and human, so that organizational objectives are achieved.

Organizations are configurations that operate in a system-like manner—they consume inputs and transform these assets into outputs such as goods and services. All the processes that operate within the system are related and interdependent. Unfortunately, however, these processes often function as independent entities with only casual regard for the codependency of system relationships. Subsequently, work is done, but in a manner that is not particularly effective or efficient.

This chapter examines a leader's role in getting the organization to function as a system in which the sum of the pieces acts as a whole in mutual dependency. The following topics are discussed:

- The organization as an open system
- Processes are the culprit, not the people
- Coordinating and controlling processes
- The leader's role

The Organization as an Open System

An organization is the sum of many processes working together under the restraint of environmental influences to achieve a particular purpose. Organizations are an amalgamation of human and material resources—people, raw materials, facilities, equipment, methods, and money—that are managed and deployed to produce outcomes. Because outcomes are achieved through the application of labor—human endeavor— organizations are also social enterprises that interact with their surrounding environment. The organization is part of an open system that receives environmental inputs and converts them into outputs that are consumed by the environment. These relationships are illustrated in Figure 2.1.

All components in the system are linked in a series of codependent relationships. Optimization can happen only when all adjoining processes and components are considered and evaluated as potential opportunities for improvement. Meddling with one part of the system at the disadvantage of others will produce only second-rate results. The leader's success under this arrangement is contingent on an ability

Inputs	Throughputs	Outputs
Money Materials People Facilities Equipment Methods Social and political ideas	**Organizational Processes** Planning Organizing Doing and Transforming Controlling Upgrading and Improving	Distribution of products and services Customer service Community service Advertising Political influence

Figure 2.1   The organization as part of an open system.

to respond to both organizational factors and environmental factors and harmonize competing influences. The following thoughts on the topic are adapted from Deming (1994, p. 50):

> It is the leader's job to direct and align the efforts of all components toward the system's purpose. A system will not manage itself. When left to themselves, components can become selfish, competitive, and independent profit centers capable of undermining and destroying the system. The leader's aim should be cooperation among components toward the system's purpose. Everyone in the system must understand the danger and loss to an organization that can occur from unrestrained competition and efforts at single-component improvement without regard for the whole system.

In the following example, one part of the system was maximized at the expense of other system components:

> This particular division of a large power-products manufacturer had no in-house manufacturing capability. To be precise, all manufactured parts, hardware, and some subassemblies were purchased from outside suppliers. The final product, however, was assembled at several rural facilities in the United States under corporate ownership where there was a wage advantage.
>
> When problems arose at assembly with fit-up, size, finish, or cleanliness of parts—which seemed to be continual—placing responsibility was often difficult because parts were

multisourced and mixed when inventoried. Even with a robust incoming inspection program, nonconforming parts crept into the supply chain. Subsequently, compromises at assembly were made to accommodate the continual need for finished units. Without regard for difficulties, production had to be kept running because there was ongoing pressure to make shipments.

Corrective action usually meant working at the supplier's production site. The effort entailed inspecting parts and providing assistance that would improve the supplier's processes and capability. However, after hours of collaborative effort, there was no guarantee that a supplier would remain the vendor of choice over an extended period. Routinely, the same parts would appear on the corrective action report because purchasing had shifted to a new source, thus forcing assembly functions to make adjustments and resolve what appeared to be a recurring issue. The job of problem solving became a repeat exercise, usually miles from the assembly operation but at different locations and with new sets of players.

Purchasing in this situation was tasked with reducing costs. The department manager received a semiannual bonus based on documented savings. Purchasing agents were reviewed and promoted based on their ability to reduce supplier costs. There was little concern for the varying inconsistency and reliability of purchased items. In fact, the quality department and manufacturing engineering were ridiculed by purchasing as overzealous nitpickers who should be focusing on the poor performance of assembly workers.

The director of operations responsible for these facilities often overrode decisions that favored efforts toward process consistency and the reduction of supplier inconsistency. The goal was production at the lowest cost and keeping operations running regardless of conditions. He viewed such attempts at problem solving as expensive nonessential activities and cited continual problems at assembly as failures by the quality department and manufacturing engineering to do their job. The problem, he pronounced, was not ensuring inputs but getting the process to work in spite of irregularities. After all, the current method for managing suppliers was saving big dollars.

Unfortunately, the notion of indulging one portion of a system at the disadvantage of another—all in the name of cost savings—did not change until declining sales and a reputation for poor quality forced the ouster of the director of operations. This failure, by the next level of management, to appreciate the organization as a system containing codependent processes became costly for the parent company in terms of not only reputation and lost sales but also overall production costs. If manufacturing engineering and the quality department had been allowed to manage process inconsistency and establish a preferred supplier list based on vendor performance, losses from scrap, rework, downtime, and problem-solving travel would have been greatly reduced.

The organization was not viewed as an open system. Everyone from supplier to production, assembly, distribution, and finally the customer lost something in this example. Each part of the system was allowed to maximize its survival at the expense of others. Competition and a misguided focus on one set of cost-saving variables nearly sunk this product line. Not recognizing organizational dependencies was a costly mistake. Similarly, recent problems at foreign and many domestic automotive companies are one more case in point where maximizing some processes—portions of the system—for self-preservation and reward at the expense of the whole system can lead to enormous losses.

Processes Are the Culprit, Not the People

More than once, I am sure you have heard the remark, "This would be easy if it weren't for the people involved." Yes, people can be emotional and contentious, but usually there is a reason. Work groups and individuals are often the first place problem solvers look when trying to assign blame for system or process issues. These employees know that the tendency to be cited as culprits for process or system problems is unjust, particularly when other factors often appear as more likely candidates and bigger contributors to failure. Because of repeated scapegoating and conditioning, the workforce will try to keep its head down and stay out of the way, often repeating the catchphrase, "That's not my problem." Pointing the finger at hapless individuals because they are close at hand is human nature, but it is a losing proposition in terms of both finding a solution and human relations.

Both Joseph Juran (1995) and W. Edwards Deming (1986), through their studies, found that the bulk (80 to 96 percent) of system and process problems are beyond the control of individuals and work groups. Specifically, the vast majority of problems are the result of materials, methods, machinery, equipment, funding, policies, and management itself. All are process components over which the workforce has little or no control. So, fixating on people, who have only 4 percent responsibility or at most maybe 20 percent, is really an unproductive strategy. This perhaps may seem to be a preemptive and decisive notion, but nevertheless it is a misguided and deeply flawed idea; resolution will remain elusive and issues will recur because root causes have not been confronted.

Take, for instance, this country's public schools. Most people seem to agree that many school systems are in trouble. Students are dropping out at unacceptable rates, and those who stay are often deficient in a wide range of subjects. However, rather than considering these systems as a larger set of related processes—the school board, the funding, the principals and administrators, the lack of public support, the disengaged parents, the poor facilities, the lack of materials, and the political maliciousness that might be at work— teachers are singled out as the main reason for failure. Even though, after years of mandated schemes to remediate alleged teacher deficiencies—student testing, incentives, charter schools, teacher training, and downright dismissal—nothing has really changed.

Study after study has shown that these efforts have failed to raise student scores and stem the dropout rate significantly. Instead, system after system has figured out how to compromise requirements and undermine criteria so outcomes appear to be improving. The public has been asked to accept anecdotal evidence, presented by political antagonists interested in unraveling the public system, that public schools have failed. The social agenda and real goal, in this case, are schools run for profit, the establishment of private institutions that compete against community-supported and controlled schools to funnel a portion of public tax dollars into some individual's private pocket, including a hefty profit. The justification, of course, is that quality will be improved. But, that will not happen because the system is working against itself. Free enterprise, as these political pundits envision it, creates winners and losers. Some schools will do well, while others will fail miserably. The losers presumably will be closed, and the winners will be replicated. But, that is not how it has worked. Typically, taxpayers have been asked to fix the problem, pick up the tab, and bail out the failed institutions, both public and private. Does this sound familiar?

As long as problems are personalized—not looked at in the broader context of *what* rather than *who*—true and lasting resolutions are not going to be found. Trying to make one part of the system accountable without considering other equally important factors is a losing game. Pointing the finger at people is not a strategy for success. It produces low yields with calls to visit some problems repeatedly. Big gains come from looking at the whole system and finding those points where improvements can be made that will be lasting and permanent and will produce a sizable return for all stakeholders. Accordingly, "Management and leadership have another job, namely, to govern for the future, and not become victims of their own circumstances" (Deming, 1994, p. 54).

Shortly after World War II, and based on his work during that period, Juran (1954, 1995) described the importance of separating the vital few from the useful many by a universal sorter called the Pareto principle. In this condition, a very small number of items typically generate the largest opportunity for substantial gain. It is based on studies done by the Italian economist Vilfredo Pareto, who observed that a few people controlled most of the wealth in a majority of economies. For example, the top 4 percent of households in the United States control nearly 80 percent of the country's wealth. This phenomenon, by which a few significant events dominate, Juran (1995) said, held true for many other situations. The following are several of his examples:

■ Of the 500 items cataloged in inventory at a particular company, 25 (or only 5 percent) of the items accounted for 72 percent of the dollars.
■ A company with 389 customers found that 10 percent of these customers accounted for 66 percent of the sales income.
■ In a machine tool company, 2 of the 15 departments contributed to over 50 percent of the scrap and rework, and one complex part was the cause of half the loss.
■ In an analysis of a company's maintenance costs, 6 percent of the work resulted in 83 percent of repair charges.

Although each of the vital few items is unique and important, there are implications or considerations for finding and dealing with causes that have the best chance of returning substantial rewards. This concept is reflected in the following statements:

■ Problem solving will typically uncover several significant causes.
■ Each is usually system interdependent.
■ Making uninformed judgments based on potential return without study will not produce a solution.

- Finding and focusing on key constraints—the vital few—will produce substantial gain and allow the trivial many to be addressed and possibly treated as a single class of problem.
- Each significant cause will require study to determine an appropriate solution.

Problems are not resolved through single-handed heroic action that creates winners and losers. Each cause has interdependencies that should be studied and assessed for an approach that is best for the whole system. Results are not found simply by reviewing reports, doing analysis, and then making pronouncements. Meaningful answers necessitate performing investigation and fact-finding, asking questions, and getting others involved in decision making. Discovering and implementing the right solution often requires experimentation and compromise. Problem solving needs to be a search for answers that produces win-win solutions that do not pit one part of the system against another for individual work unit gain.

Unfortunately, there are organizational practices that make thinking in terms of an integral and unified system difficult for managers and leaders. First and foremost is the pressure for short-term gain. This shifts the focus from customers to getting product out the door and into the market. Individual production units scramble to compete for resources that will enhance their ability and reputation as contributors to product flow. In such a competitive atmosphere, there is no sense of responsibility for the entire system, or even customers, only the individual work unit. Organizational goals and system-wide plans become background noise that is overlooked in favor of divisional or departmental objectives.

When organizational or system problems arise, there is a tendency to focus on events as a unique occurrence—as a snapshot—rather than a probable series of actions that are separated in time and interdependent. System thinking requires a broad perspective in which problem solving searches for cause-and-effect relationships that have been studied over time. One data point does not predict a trend or reveal a plausible solution to a problem that is due to a cascade of events. Solutions cannot be found by short-term thinking or looking for the quick fix, but by viewing situations as multiple events that are linked but separated by time. In system thinking, individuals are not the first and sole consideration for problems when larger opportunities are more likely to be found in the dynamic complexities of the system itself. System thinking is an orderly and disciplined approach for examining and managing the organization as an integral part of an open, vigorous, complex system that has many players and numerous contingencies.

Coordinating and Controlling Processes

Moving an organization toward its intended goals and ultimate purpose will oblige the leader to harmonize organizational preferences for stability as well as change. Stability is needed because it provides a constancy of purpose that is reassuring and allows people to function effectively and efficiently under a complex array of demands. Change is desired because it allows the organization to adapt, accommodate, and survive environmental instabilities as well as competition. This balancing act will require the coordination of functional units and the control of diverse activities.

Coordination

Coordination can be defined as the integration of work activities and goals from separate functions so the organization is a coherent and efficient entity capable of operating successfully within the larger system. The primary mechanism used to facilitate coordination is structure. Organizational structure divides work into manageable chunks so individual workers are able to contribute meaningful effort toward the enterprise's goals. In addition, structure collects work functions into similar or logical groupings and departmentalizes effort toward common goals. In essence, the organization's structure systematizes work activities and defines how activities are operationally linked in terms of reporting relationships. Both formal and informal methods operate within the organization's structure, which further characterizes how work will be accomplished. These include the following organizational influences:

■ *Culture:* The norms, values, and beliefs of individuals and work groups
■ *Grapevine:* The informal communication system that is built around personal relationships and individual contact
■ *Policies, procedures, rules, and work instructions:* Written documentation that guides work activities and their administration
■ *Management information system:* The official record-keeping system that gathers, organizes, records, and disperses information that is necessary for managing the organization
■ *Committees and task forces:* Groups that facilitate problem solving and allow different parts of the organization to work together in a common effort

Unfortunately, as work becomes divided and often more specialized, people in work units typically develop their own particular sense of purpose and how to proceed and contribute to the organization's overall goals. Although departmentalization and specialization help the organization manage and utilize resources more efficiently, the need for supervision and oversight tends to increase. The division of work brings with it problems that make achieving effective coordination somewhat difficult. The leader's job becomes one of integration— getting people to work together in a cooperative manner for the common good.

The leader's primary tool in this case will be communication. Coordination in a modern enterprise is dependent on the need for gathering, processing, and dispersing information—communication. The second tool is the managerial hierarchy: the formal structure and how it is populated by executives, managers, and supervisors. The levels and reporting relationships are usually defined by an organizational chart and shaped by how the enterprise wants to approach its markets and manage resources to accommodate market demand. These two components directly under the leader's control can have significant influence on organizational performance. Both communication and structure are malleable and can be shaped to help improve performance and achieve overall goals.

Communication flows both vertically and horizontally within the organization. The vertical information structure is usually electronic in nature and was developed to assist planning, coordination, and control by gathering and dispersing financial, production, and marketing information. The horizontal communication system, on the other hand, tends to be built on relationships. In this case, transfer methods include direct contact or boundary-spanning roles such as coordinators, committees, task forces, and cross-functional teams. These two areas of coordination—communication and hierarchy—can be addressed and managed using the following approaches:

- Develop and communicate the organization's purpose, including vision, mission, and values. Be clear about the organization's short-term and long-term direction and indicate performance expectations for balancing customer needs with other stakeholder needs.
- Be explicit with executives and senior managers on how they should communicate values, direction, and expectations throughout the organization to all employees.
- Set expectations and assess how executives and senior managers create a working environment for

empowerment, innovation, nimbleness, and employee as well as organizational learning.

■ Set the example by living up to the values and expectations that have been advocated and promoted. A leader can undermine credibility and workforce commitment by displaying duplicitous behavior.

Control

Coordination is focused on bringing together the actions of organizational units and individuals; control is concerned with making sure outputs and actions meet expectations. Control starts by setting expectations—creating a benchmark—then measuring result against criterion and initiating corrective action if there is a mismatch. As with coordination, most of the means for control within work units are the responsibility of managers and supervisors. However, as the leader you are ultimately responsible for organizational outcomes and will need to assess executives and senior managers on their ability to create and monitor strategies, methods, and processes that really work and that meet goals and expectations.

The need for control is a fact of life. It is part of the production cycle, the learning cycle, and, as it is sometimes characterized, the Deming Cycle (Plan, Do, Study, Act [PDSA]). Control is a component of study and act. This is the place where decisions are made regarding adequacy of component processes or larger system performance. Here, an action for improvement is shaped based on evaluation against an expected outcome. Control is the decision point, the motivating force that drives learning and continuous improvement. Without the problem solving and corrective action that control encourages, an organization would not be able to make advantageous modifications in response to prevailing conditions and would be quickly overwhelmed by environmental complexities. Several factors make the need for control and the ability to make corrections rapidly an essential task. These conditions include the need for delegation, the pressure for more organizational sophistication, the impact of errors and mistakes, and the need to adapt and change.

As the leader, you have delegated both authority and responsibility to executives and senior managers. In turn, they have likewise leveraged themselves through delegation so the nitty-gritty details or work are done. However, accountability has not been diminished, so there needs to be some way for assessing if subordinates are indeed accomplishing desired outcomes. Without control, delegation would be a waiting game, possibly one of chance.

The organization and the larger business system it functions within are multifaceted. Product lines and services are typically segmented and specialized, plants and facilities can be geographically separated, and the workforce can be multinational with cultural differences. Managing and controlling can be difficult and often require close monitoring so individual units function efficiently and effectively. Control ensures that individual units are functioning in alignment with overall organizational goals.

The unanticipated happens, plans fail, costs are out of line, and new products misfire—mistakes are made. Problems big and small are just part of organizational life. Control mechanisms can catch issues before they become catastrophic, can provide an opportunity for learning and recovery, and can ensure the uniform consistency of products and services.

The environmental and system conditions under which the organization operates are by disposition strong-willed forces. New regulations are enacted, new materials and processes are discovered, new products and services are invented, and consequently new markets emerge or established markets shift. Change is just part of doing business; it is inevitable. An effective system of assessment and control can be the front line in detecting changes, such as abnormal variability in demand, or the failure to adjust to emerging conditions, such as increasing costs. Control is the management function that permits rapid adaptation to change, which brings both opportunities as well as threats.

Control must also have a standard, based on measurement, against which actions can be evaluated so corrective steps can be taken if results do not meet expectations. The measurement process will require both consideration and decision to determine what might be measured to trigger the call for action. Kaplan and Norton (1996), in their book *The Balanced Scorecard*, suggest the subsequent four business areas for measurement and assessment of conditions:

- *Financial:* This perspective measures the ultimate results of business activity and ability to compensate shareholders. Included are profitability, revenue growth, return on investment, economic value added, and shareholder value.
- *Internal business processes:* This perspective focuses attention on activities and processes that drive organizational success. Included here are items such as quality, productivity, operating costs, and time-dependent cycles, such as delay, waiting, and production.
- *Learning and growth:* This perspective focuses attention on human resources and process adaptability. Included are skill development, innovation, market development, intellectual property, and employee satisfaction.
- *Customer:* This perspective places attention on customer needs and satisfaction. Included are repeat business, satisfaction ratings, and indicators of service. Customers typically evaluate service in terms of reliability, tangibles, assurance, empathy, and responsiveness.

Kaplan and Norton's (1996) balanced scorecard works well because it considers multiple business areas. Too often, the focus is just on financial aspects and the profits that are generated. Unfortunately, when assessment is single minded, results and rewards will favor what is being measured and neglect other important factors. The outcomes will probably meet expectations, but usually for only a short period. Eventually, there will be a collapse because other sustaining functions have been neglected or gutted. A broad set of performance measurements that provides an all-inclusive system view is preferable. The Malcolm Baldrige criteria provide another, but similar, perspective on organizational assessment. Included are these four areas: (1) customers, (2) market and financial, (3) human resources, and (4) organizational effectiveness.

Next discussed is still another model for organizational assessment based on the interaction of enterprise activities and how they influence one another. Figure 2.2 illustrates this cascade of influences and the direction of influential flow. Leadership is the starting point and the driving force behind overall organizational success. The leader orchestrates strategy development; executives and managers rationalize organizational goals through the development of plans. In turn, the plans influence how processes will be organized and staffed, which determines the efficiency of operations and the effectiveness of people who work at producing products or services. The outputs from these organizational endeavors will be consumed and evaluated based on perceived quality. When quality meets or exceeds customer expectations, there is

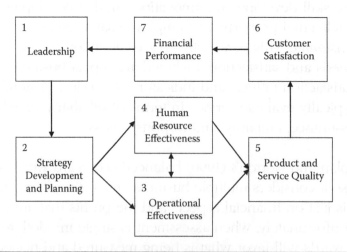

Figure 2.2 Enterprise activities and their interaction.

satisfaction and increasing business, which has a direct impact on financial performance. The quality of financial measures provides feedback that directly influences leadership decision making.

Each of the activities (Boxes 2 through 6 in Figure 2.2) has indicators that can be used to assess its individual effectiveness. These indicators (see the material in the final section of this chapter) provide an early warning system that can initiate corrective action and increase overall organizational effectiveness. The limits or standards of measurement for each indicator depend on the type of business or enterprise. Usually, measurements are driven by customer expectations but can be influenced by market factors, competition, economic forces, and the normal capability of organizational processes. Deciding what should be measured and determining the limits or tolerances for each measure are part of strategy development and the dialogue during executive decision making.

Table 2.1 is a list of indicators categorized by activity. This is by no means a definitive list. Since each organization is unique, other measures can be developed that are appropriate to the market or prevailing circumstances. However, since measurement, tracking, and analysis are tedious and expensive, care should be taken to look for indicators that truly measure effectiveness against proposed organizational objectives. Probably no more than two or three indicators are need in each category.

Assessment is a multilevel responsibility and practice. Executives, managers, supervisors, and employees should be making decisions about their own work processes based on solid information backed by actual data. As the leader, you need to decide for yourself which key measures will be your indicators for organizational health. Again, do not focus exclusively on the financial dimensions. These are an after-the-fact gauge. Other activities are precursory and contributors to financial results. Look for indicators that will provide an early warning and create a more robust picture of organizational

Table 2.1 Assessment Indicators

1. Strategy Development and Planning
  • Plans met
  • Special requests met
  • New products or services developed
  • Elapsed time for development
  • Requests for deviation or change
  • Project costs
  • Estimated project cost vs. actual costs
2. Operational Effectiveness
  • Units shipped
  • Items processed
  • Productivity
  • Cycle time
  • Down time
  • Scrap and rework costs
  • Error rate
  • Damage costs
  • Operating costs
  • Maintenance costs
3. Human Resource Effectiveness
  • Employee turnover
  • Employee satisfaction and morale
  • Skills developed
  • Health and safety costs
  • Training costs
  • Overtime costs
  • Unethical practices found
	4. Product and Service Quality
	  • Number of blemishes
	  • Number of rejects
	  • Delay time
	  • Waiting time
	  • On-time deliveries
	  • Requests met
	  • Repair and replacement costs
	  • Warranty costs
	5. Customer Satisfaction
	  • Customer complaints
	  • Customer retention
	  • Customer satisfaction ratings
	  • Returns
	  • Legal actions taken
	6. Financial Performance
	  • Market share
	  • Return on investment
	  • Profits
	  • Shareholder value

vitality. Likewise, executives, managers, and supervisors should be establishing a set of key measures for the processes under their responsibility. Kaplan and Norton (1996) suggest this subject is worth executive discussion, and that a set of harmonizing organization-wide measures be developed and deployed. Performance standards that have relevance and meaning should involve input by others. When standards are set by one person, there is a good chance a criterion will be considered impractical or unreasonable by others who are asked to test for compliance and assess results.

Deming (1986, p. 277) suggested that measurement standards or operational definitions should contain the following elements:

- A criterion or standard
- A test for compliance to the criterion
- A decision rule for interpreting test results

For example, a fast-food restaurant chain sets a criterion for one of its objectives: Waiting time during peak periods should be less than 5 minutes. The test for compliance might be several time studies of 30 patrons during the mealtime crush. A decision rule for action in this case might be the following: If more than 5 percent of the test subjects take longer than 5 minutes, begin an investigation to uncover the causes for delay.

Another example is a community college with a population of roughly 25,000 students. It has set a strategic goal for increasing full-time equivalent (FTE) students—the number of students taking 12 credits based on total enrollment credits divided by 12—a calculation often used to determine state aid. A review of the past 10 years showed the average range for variability from semester to semester was 200 full-time students, and overall enrollments had steadily increased by nearly 2,000 full-time students during that time. The goal or standard in this case was another 1,000 FTE students over the next 5 years, or a 200-FTE student increase annually. The test for compliance was closeness to the straight-line increase of 1,000 FTE students over the next 5 years. The decision rule—the trigger for problem solving—was total enrolled FTE students plotted against the anticipated increase.

Of course, this led to a discussion about when to act—after one semester's data or after several semesters' cumulative data. The subsequent discussion illustrates the dilemma often confronted when creating decision rules and trying to accommodate the influence of normal variation on process indicators. When is the time to take action and begin the search for answers? Acting too soon can create a lot of hand-wringing over nothing; acting too late can mean difficulty in picking up the pieces and making the situation whole again.

Typically, there is a tendency to think in terms of absolutes: This month's sales figures were below last month's figures, so something needs to be done. But, really, the world does not work that way. A natural ebb and flow occurs. Things are not consistently the same from day to day and month to month. There are increases and decreases. Decision rules need to take this reality into consideration because two data points do not predict a trend. It would be better to consider at least five points as a minimum for forecasting potential negative consequences. There are reasons—based on probability—for waiting to see what type of trend is developing. Chapter 5 examines variability in depth and some of the statistical theory behind it. Nevertheless, reacting in response to normal system ups and downs—often too quickly—creates unnecessary distortions that can turn a well-functioning situation into a disaster.

In the previous community college example, the vice president of academic affairs reacted to the normal downturn in enrollments without considering if indeed a trend was developing. This arbitrary reaction set off a yearlong battle among administrators, staff, and faculty that led to recriminations and allegations that the drop resulted from student unease over teaching methods. Ironically, even with all the finger-pointing and an unclear path for problem solving, the next year's head count surpassed expectations, and the issue quickly disappeared as an area of concern. However, the bitterness that remained ultimately led to the removal of the vice president and a return to a department chairmanship.

Setting a measurement standard is something that should be done with thought and discussion by all concerned parties. The decision to act should be more than an arbitrary response containing a prescribed solution that is based on opinion and hubris—the misguided notion that unwavering resolve in the absence of fact is all that is needed. On the contrary, the conclusion to move in a new direction should start with problem solving. Look at the system and the possibility of several causes. Consider the prevailing approach and how methods were deployed that created the less-than-acceptable result. Then, link conclusions to results with data that have credibility and are verifiable under scrutiny by other system stakeholders.

The Leader's Role

As indicated in the first chapter, one of the leader's tasks is alignment: bringing system stakeholders together in a common effort so organizational objectives can be achieved. Alignment happens because people understand how their work-related roles mesh with others in the organization and the larger system. The leader facilitates alignment by creating the right atmosphere—sets direction and rationalizes future possibilities—then follows up by assessing outcomes against measures.

The leader, along with executives, develops the organization's strategic goals and timelines for achieving organizational objectives. In turn, executives and managers create detailed plans and institute deployment at all levels to ensure effective and efficient work activities. In addition, a set of objective measurements is established for defining and monitoring progress. Comparative data are gathered and analyzed to assess operations and understand how organizational relationships are functioning. The information obtained is then used for decision making and to improve work structures and overall system potential.

Alignment is further achieved when executives and senior managers encourage and support skill development through worker training and the use of on-the-job learning. A well-functioning organization cannot improve or achieve high performance unless talent and ability are routinely upgraded to meet ever-changing competitive and environmental pressures. The goal should be a work environment that encourages cooperation, involvement, and joint decision making and is concerned with employee satisfaction and well-being. Human effectiveness and organizational effectiveness are linked and will determine the quality of goods and services produced. High quality in turn creates satisfied customers and ultimately high returns that will ensure continued investor confidence.

System thinking is all about relationships and how to optimize the interactions between system components. The leader's role in this setting is to guide the organization by providing vision, giving direction, and assessing outcomes. It starts by considering and balancing the needs and expectations of customers, suppliers, workers, stakeholders, and shareholders for the common good of all. When one component is allowed to exert itself at the expense of others, the system will suffer and ultimately lose its equilibrium. This creates winners and losers and can have disabling consequences for every system stakeholder. Table 2.2 summarizes the leader's role in aligning organizational units and improving the overall system.

In summary, a leader needs to understand how the organization's efforts and actions act together as a larger system. Optimizing parts of the system—for example, just the sales department's effectiveness—can have consequences

Table 2.2 The Leader's Role in Guiding and Aligning the Organization

Facilitates Direction	Assess Effectiveness
Establishes the organization's purpose and future direction.	Identifies organizational effectiveness and capability measures with the help of executives and senior managers.
Develops the organization's mission, vision, and value statements with the help of executives and senior managers.	Assesses overall organizational capability and effectiveness, then translates findings into priorities for improvement.
Ensures that the purpose, direction, and values are clearly communicated throughout the organization.	Ensures that executives and senior managers use findings to improve managerial effectiveness at all levels in the organization.
Develops and deploys tactical plans that operationalize short- and long-term strategic objectives with the help of executives and senior managers.	Ensures that findings are used to improve work unit effectiveness as well as supplier, partner, and other system stakeholder capabilities and effectiveness.
Ensures that executives and senior managers establish an environment that encourages empowerment, teamwork, innovation, and continual learning.	Considers, anticipates, and addresses the impact of organizational operations on the system and community at large.
Demonstrates behaviors that model the organization's vision and values. Exemplifies the rhetoric and assures executives and managers at all levels do the same.	Uses information about system communities to improve, support, and strengthen these associations.

and will not advance the overall system. The fallout can be catastrophic, leaving both the organization and the system mortally wounded. The current economic crisis and resulting downturn are a prime example of maximizing a portion of a system at the expense of other communities in the system. Appreciation for the system necessitates cooperation, coordination, and control, which in turn are expressed through leadership.

Deming (1994) defines a system as a network of interdependent components that work together to try to accomplish a particular aim. The system's aim is the overall defining purpose that sets it apart from others. To be successful, the purpose should drive activities that benefit everyone—customers, stockholders, employees, suppliers, community, and the environment. It is the job of leadership and component managers to guide and direct operations so that competition is minimized and everyone can work toward the common purpose.

Brian Joiner (1994) suggests leadership and management have the additional obligation of helping their organization's ability to improve. This responsibility starts with understanding: figuring out what is going on before responding by gathering the facts and studying the system—measure, experiment, and analyze. Use a rational method for problem solving and then sustain improvements by anchoring the change. Most opportunities for improvement lie within the system itself and are therefore management's responsibility. However, leveraging one system component against another will not improve the system as a whole. All elements must work in harmony. This means developing and encouraging methods based on knowledge and supported by data—facts—that can focus everyone's thinking on continual and sustained improvement that has a long-term prospective. Table 2.3 describes methods for problem solving and sustaining improvement.

Often, people think of systems in terms of organization—how elements fit together. The diagram that is typically

Table 2.3 Problem Solving Methods and Steps to Sustain Improvement

PDSA Cycle	Six Sigma	Process Improvement	Sustaining Improvement and Anchoring Change
Problem Resolution			
1. Plan 2. Do 3. Study	1. Define 2. Measure 3. Analyze	1. Define the problem 2. Describe the current situation 3. Analyze causes 4. Develop solutions	1. Explain the need for making improvements 2. Communicate a unifying purpose 3. Identify formal and informal networks and ensure their participation 4. Create a plan for action 5. Create the opportunity for small but meaningful gains 6. Empower people to take action 7. Manage resistance to system improvement 8. Complete the restructuring of daily activities 9. Sustain improvement
Solution Implementation			
4. Act	4. Improve 5. Control	5. Implement improvements 6. Evaluate results and make modifications 7. Integrate into daily work	

Source: Adapted from Schultz, J.R. (2011). *Making it all work: A pocket guide to sustain improvement and anchor change.* New York: Routledge.

drawn portrays the chain of command—an organizational chart of who reports to whom. But, a system is much more. It is a whole entity (a business, a school, a hospital) consisting of many parts. The system as a whole has a purpose, as does each component. For the system or organization to function properly, purposes must be synchronized. When purposes are inconsistent, the result will be chronic dysfunction and ineffectiveness. The leader's job is ensuring that the system is interacting as a whole.

Chapter 3

Understand Why People Behave as They Do

Introduction

Frequently, the following remark is heard: "Dealing with people and their behavior really makes this job difficult." Yet, it is the people—the workforce—who will ultimately get the job done and make things happen. So, understanding and accommodating individual behaviors is just part of the job. In most cases, people behave as they do in response to the way they are treated. People are shaped by their own world experiences and because of this conditioning will perceive and react to the organization's environment in different ways. These inherent and varied ways for operating have a common link with an individual's inclinations and preferences for learning. This means that the potential for differences of opinion are inescapable. So, as the leader you will need to develop strategies for focusing the labor force and convincing these individuals to work in the organization's common interest.

This chapter provides some insight about human nature and suggests how to use the diverse array of behaviors as a force for problem solving and growth. The following topics are covered:

- Complexity of human nature
- Group and organizational dynamics
- Conflict, competition, and cooperation
- Lessons learned

Complexity of Human Nature

Current research contains competing theories about human nature and the causes for human behavior. To a large extent, these theories agree there are intrinsic (innate) and extrinsic (environmental) factors that have an impact on and influence how individuals are going to interpret their world of work and how they will relate to others in that setting. Swiss-born psychiatrist Carl Jung suggested that although the factors influencing behavior are random, the consequences of such conduct are predictable and therefore classifiable. Not in step with his colleagues, Jung argued that the differences in behavior—individual temperament—were the result of preferences that are shaped by inherent as well as learned influences. These preferences—the way an individual perceives and evaluates the world—develop early in life and become the foundation for personality. Such preferences are the core for an individual's attractions and aversions to events, people, and tasks that are present throughout a person's life (Kroeger and Thuesen, 1992).

Ultimately, Jung's ideas for classifying people were translated and further developed by Katharine Briggs and Isabel Briggs Myers (discussed in Kroeger and Thuesen, 1992) as an approach for measuring preferences and describing individual behaviors. Myers's and Briggs's studies (Center for Applications of Psychological Type, 2012) and resulting methodology produced four pairs of opposing tendencies or eight alternative preferences. Accordingly, people are either

■ Extraverted or introverted
■ Sensing or intuitive
■ Thinking or feeling
■ Judging or perceiving

This pairing produced 16 distinct personality types; this is interesting, but of course not the only method for organizing and classifying individual behaviors. Yet, it does provide some insight into personality development and the number of individual temperaments that might be found in the workplace.

In addition, people bring competencies (abilities) and attitudes (values) to the workplace. These individual differences—temperament, abilities, and values—influence workplace performance and the feeling of fulfillment that people derive from work. This means that all three factors should be managed and aided, often individually, if desired levels of accomplishment are to be realized. Each of these characteristics has the potential for moderating individual work behavior. However, trying to manipulate any single factor with the hope of changing behavior is going to be difficult and may in fact create unintentional aftereffects.

Consequently, a number of interesting, but controversial, approaches have been developed to control human behavior. Many of these are based on the assumption that reward and punishment are strong motivators and, if applied correctly, will shape and modify conduct to improve performance. Behavior modification is grounded on the notion that rewarding desired outcomes will produce repeated acceptable behavior, and punishing undesirable outcomes will extinguish unacceptable behavior. This implies that manipulating the consequences of behavior will change the behavior itself. However, for reward or punishment to have an impact, the incentive must have relevance—be considered desirable, equitable, and timely by the individual receiving the reinforcement. As a result, this approach usually fails because consequences are often neither timely nor relevant. Frequently, attempts at modification are blatant abuses of power that are provocative, coercive, and perceived as flagrantly unfair. Yet, research does indicate that incentives and disincentives can produce compliance, but these competing forces do not have a lasting impact on behavior. Once the stimulus is withdrawn, people will do what they want to do. In addition, techniques that are deemed as punitive or negative can encourage resentment and pushback at some future date. Using methods that are more supportive in approach, though seemingly limited in ability to reform, does not come with the same risk for reprisal. Table 3.1 lists four methods commonly used to modify behavior.

Although these techniques may have some impact, the overall work situation, including policies, production systems, supervision, and the culture, tends to play a more influential role. These effects interact with the individual's need for achievement, affiliation, and power to create feelings and attitudes that cannot be easily reshaped using reward and punishment. Many studies found that the work situation and the impression of peer groups have a larger influence on individual disposition and performance than prizes or punishment—carrots or the stick.

In his book *Punish by Rewards*, Alfie Kohn (1993) points out that the use of positive and negative motivators often has unintended consequences. As an example, using money and bonuses to drive improved performance can lead to distortions that disenfranchise customers and may ultimately collapse the reputation of a business. The focus shifts from serving customers and stakeholders to preserving the system for rewards; self-interest becomes the focus. The recent economic downturn—a striking case—was driven by concerns for individual gain and not the customer or overall sustainability of the financial system and the housing market. Coincidently,

Table 3.1 Behavior Modification Methods

Method	Strategy	Tactic
Positive Reinforcement	Provide reinforcements that are perceived as desirable, pleasurable, and equitable to promote the replication of desired behavior	• Praise or compliments • Certificates and awards • Promotion or move to a desired position • Raise, bonus, or other economic incentives
Punishment	Apply coercive and punitive reinforcers to deter perceived unacceptable behavior	• Criticism • Manipulation—covertly distort information and restrict resources • Power use—blatantly threaten consequences • Reduce pay and bonuses • Demotion
Avoidance learning	Provide counseling that defines desirable and undesirable behavior coupled with reward and punishment to change behavior	• Provide training along with counseling or mentoring • Explain what is required and propose alternative behaviors, then praise desired behavior and admonish undesired behavior
Extinction	Remove environmental influences that may be encouraging unacceptable behavior	• Counsel coworkers on how to treat errant individual • Separate worker from power base • Move worker to new job or location • Stop reinforcing an individual's particular behaviors

the reputation for poor quality that has plagued the U.S. auto industry was driven by the notion of quantity over quality— that quality costs money. The workforce was rewarded handsomely for speed—high rates of production without a lot of concern for how work was done or what the consumer received. The idea was to get product out the door whatever it takes—slick marketing and advertising can take care of the deficiencies. "Rewards and punishments are not opposites at all; they are two sides of the same coin. And it is a coin that does not buy very much" (Kohn, 1993, p. 50). Trying to compensate for the inherent limitations of punishment and reward, other researchers have introduced ideas that move beyond basic behavior modification and deal with needs, expectations, and equity.

Accordingly, the needs theorists speculate that individual behavior is driven by unfulfilled needs—both physical and psychological. In Abraham Maslow's (1970) view, these needs are (1) biological, (2) safety, (3) social, (4) esteem, and (5) self-fulfillment. In Alderfer's (1972) case, these desires are (1) existence needs, (2) relatedness needs, and (3) growth needs. Finally, McClelland (1961) feels the drivers are the (1) need for achievement, (2) need for affiliation, and (3) need for power. Each of the theories, even though the terminology differs, speculates that if the organization can administer and manage its work environment toward the fulfillment of needs, then everything will be just fine. While there is considerable evidence to support the relationship between needs achievement and performance, there is little practical guidance on how these ideas should be implemented in a complex work setting. Trying to measure the significance or influence of any particular need has been difficult. Research has not defined the importance of various needs, but there is some support for the notion that needs have a hierarchy and should be filled in a specific order. As with behavior modification, only a small part of the human relations spectrum is being manipulated. Results are going to be better in most cases, but not overwhelmingly so and probably not repeatedly over the long term, particularly if other situational factors are not viewed as positive.

Another approach to improving job performance is equity theory. It is supported by the concept of fairness, that job performance and satisfaction are the result of conscious evaluation between rewards and punishment in comparison to what others are receiving. If there is perceived equity about workplace management—pay, promotion, work assignments, work conditions, access to resources, and supervision—then performance will be high. If, on the other hand, there is sensed inequity—others are getting a better deal—then performance will be low. Or, in some cases, if inequity is perceived to be excessive, the resulting reaction may be unrest with bickering, strife, or work stoppage and outright hostility. A collective feeling of inequity can have corrosive and destructive effects on the workplace. The theory further predicts that when people feel unjustly treated, they will demand larger compensations to restore a sense of equity. This is a lesson that many enterprises have failed to learn. Inequity is a larger motivator than equity and will inevitably lead to pushback. Fairness and mechanisms for addressing injustice should be a consideration when developing any management strategy that tries to improve organizational performance.

The last theory offered for consideration is the idea that individuals will weigh effort and level of performance against outcomes based on expectations. In other words, if a person expects a particular result (in terms of both satisfaction and compensation because of effort) and the outcome matches prospects, then performance will be high. However, if anticipated outcomes do not match expectations, then future performance will be lowered to agree with probable realities. In this model, there can be multiple levels of expectancy—a number of hoped-for outcomes—and varying levels of expected satisfaction. Consequently, performance is not a constant, but a changeable factor that is the result of perceived value. Behavior, effort, and resulting performance are determined by a combination of organizational and environmental forces: past experiences, types of work, group affiliations, and supervisory interactions. In response, individuals will make conscious decisions about how to interact, respond, and perform based on the expectation that a particular behavior will produce a desired result. This means that leaders and managers must be more discerning and individually focused in their approach when dealing with people in the workplace. Understanding individual needs is a primary consideration for maintaining and improving overall organizational performance. It is the little things—sensitivities to individual needs—that often count.

So, what are the leadership implications? What can be generalized to supporting and managing human behavior? First and foremost, all of these models produce insights that contribute to the understanding of why people behave as they do. The different organizational forces become mixed to produce an effect that influences individual performance and satisfaction. It is safe to assume that individual attributes, needs, and expectations, along with task complexity, native ability, peer influence, and organizational support determine the amount of work effort that will be exerted to produce outcomes. However, in many cases the drivers—those qualities that influence behavior—are beyond the individual worker's control, particularly in a workplace setting where so many aspects of decision making are at the discretion of management. If management holds most of the power, the organization should try to create an environment that is responsive to individual needs and expectations.

When workers are asked what conditions would make their job easier, a variety of suggestions is the result. The responses cluster around a couple of ideas and place responsibility for job performance with those who are in control—managers and leaders. First, employees feel they do not need to be under continual surveillance. Instead, managers should watch for problems and then help people in the workforce solve

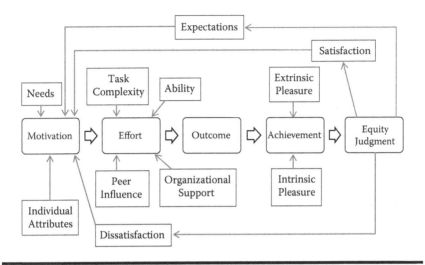

Figure 3.1   Integrated model for performance output.

them; make problem solving part of the job. Second, keep employees informed. Provide the information and feedback that is needed to keep work on track. Tell people what they are doing right, let them know what needs to improve, and then jointly decide how to make improvements. Figure 3.1 is an integrated framework that combines all of the theories previously discussed and illustrates the many influences affecting behavior.

The structure for this integrated model has at its core the basic fulfillment approach to motivation. The archetype says needs—having to pay the mortgage or the obligation to complete a task—drive actions (effort) that produce an output, thus giving a certain level of achievement (both intrinsic and extrinsic), which in turn creates an equity judgment producing feedback that adds to those feelings that influence motivation. Simply put, individuals have many needs and will try to satisfy them through effort. If the action produces an acceptable level of satisfaction, then the effort will be repeated. On the other hand, if the action produces dissatisfaction, then the effort will not be repeated with the same vigor, or the attempt may be abandoned altogether. The following are some considerations to keep in mind when trying to manage and influence behavior in an organizational setting:

- People come to work with innate attributes, individual needs, and individual expectations. Individual attributes, characteristics, and desires cannot be easily manipulated, but those factors that influence effort are affected by organizational conditions and managerial behaviors.
- Contrary to popular belief, people cannot be motivated by others. Motivation is self-initiated and contingent on individual attributes, needs, expectations, and personal judgments about equity and satisfaction.
- People can be manipulated (told), rewarded (bribed), or coerced (intimidated), but these approaches do not motivate. They produce compliance where continuing relations between levels of authority may become adversarial.
- Reward systems will accomplish what is rewarded, but not what is wanted. Concern for others—customers, constituents, or stakeholders—and the level of quality will always be sacrificed for the reward incentive.
- Organizational practices—policies, procedures, instructions, and rules—can not only hamper but also improve effort and increase output when administered with the individual's well-being in mind.
- Work itself should be made intrinsically fulfilling and rewarding. To create this reality, jobs can be designed with the offer of variety and challenge in mind. In addition, there must be a clear understanding of objectives, expected outcomes, and how performance will be measured.
- Feedback on performance that is accurate, truthful, and supporting will strengthen performance.
- Equity (fairness) is a value that should be reflected in the workplace culture, and there should be mechanisms in place that provide recourse for injustice.

■ Programs that strengthen an individual's capability and remove barriers, including inadequate tools, lack of resources, and inefficient conditions, will increase performance and the resulting output.

■ Practices that actively engage individuals in decision making about workplace improvements and workplace conditions have a positive impact on performance and consequential output.

When managerial and leadership style consists of extrinsic motivators (incentives and rewards), controlling people's behaviors, or exhorting them to work harder and smarter, then power becomes the basis for workplace relationships. The long-term result of this strategy often produces the opposite effect. People hunker down and do only what needs to be done and sometimes less. Getting them onboard, proficient, and willing to do their best requires a different approach. Accordingly, Kohn (1993) advocates three fundamental schemes for creating authentic workplace momentum. These can be thought of as the three Cs of motivation: collaboration, content, and choice.

Collaboration, of course, implies working together, not only at the work group level where people are often expected to function as a team, but also at the interface between leader and follower, where conditions affecting workplace operations are made. When people are able to work together in a cooperative relationship, they are more likely to be excited about their work. The exchange of talent and resources that occurs, and the emotional support provided through social interaction, creates enthusiasm and a sense of belonging. People will see themselves as part of a group that is committed to a collective effort that is focused on both customer happiness and stakeholder well-being.

Content in this case means a concern for the work itself. People will not be motivated if the job they are doing is drudgery and holds no interest for them. Indifference and irresponsibility are the expected response to work that is viewed as meaningless. A good job, on the other hand, offers the chance to engage in something that has resonance and satisfies the need for achievement. Work must be more than just enjoyable; it must seem worthwhile and important. It should tie the worker and the product produced or the service provided to the larger community. Work should not only be fun but also make a difference in the worker's mind-set. Creating the right environment means helping workers find the right fit—locating a position or shaping a position that is interesting and challenging.

Choice, in this context, means having the freedom to make decisions about how tasks will be carried out. Loss of autonomy creates a sense of apathy because people recognize the futility of their position—that they are powerless and subject to capricious demands with no means for recourse. People are more motivated when they can participate in decisions about goals and how the underlying objectives will be accomplished. People are more enthusiastic and driven when they can exercise a certain level of self-determination over how work should be done. When problems arise or conditions change, the work group would like to be part of the problem-solving and decision-making processes. To put it another way, when people are given responsibility for and control over their own work, the workplace becomes more democratic. This in many cases means rethinking workplace fundamentals and how people are involved and managed.

Here is an additional thought on the complexity of human behavior. The real work in any enterprise ultimately is done by the workforce: the people in the offices and on the shop floor. Empowering their effort—giving these individuals the ability to make decisions and to a large extent control the conditions that affect their social structures and ability to perform—will definitely improve the quality and quantity of work. Research has shown that the capacity to exercise control does enhance results. Think about it: Work has the three main components of planning, doing, and controlling. Traditionally, these elements were at the discretion of the individual worker. Even today, the self-employed and entrepreneurs capably manage most aspects of their own work. However, in many organizational settings, planning and controlling are at the discretion of management, and the workforce only works. The natural cycle has been disrupted. The job has become fragmented and unchallenging—thinking, decision making, creativity, and the ability to self-correct have been removed. The individual has been disempowered.

Empowerment is the process of power sharing. In the usual context, authority for getting something done is divided between a work group and its supervision. This is a relationship in which members are granted authority to make changes and accept responsibility for decisions related to their actions. Empowerment implies those in charge must be willing to share authority, and those empowered must be willing to step forward and accept the challenge. Three components sustain empowerment and must be maintained to make it work: a defined direction, freedom to make choices, and sufficient support to complete assignments.

Direction provides the boundaries for action by classifying the intent as well as results expected. Definitions include desired outcomes, measurements for results, and any other information that makes clear what the deliverable will be. Freedom allows the work group to choose methods for achieving results and applying skills to complete the job. This is guided by a clear definition for authority and responsibility. However, within that latitude people are allowed to do what is necessary without being second-guessed. Support means providing the resources necessary to get the job done. Included would be essential equipment, materials, information, people, and training. In addition, this suggests those in the leadership position must become mentors, collaborators, and partners in the process of improving performance.

Empowerment is built on trust. Power sharing implies that decisions made by a work group should not be reversed without their advice and input. A relationship of this nature facilitates collective learning and supports the group's position by sending a message of respect. Restrained oversight allows work groups to resolve issues and fix the consequences of their actions. What follows are methods that support empowerment and advance the process of self-direction:

■ Make sure there is a clear purpose and direction.
■ Ensure skills are sufficient by providing training so people are capable of operating in the current environment.
■ Be willing to place responsibility for the fundamental details of getting work done in the hands of process operators and their informal leaders who have the will and capability to complete work activities.
■ Ensure that decisions by work groups are not reversed without member consultation and consent.
■ Provide a mechanism for addressing injustices and political clout to deal with power structures that may undercut the work group's ability to engage freely in work activities.

Efforts to implement empowerment can begin to unravel when those empowered are kept in the dark. Individuals in charge, fearing loss of control, often create formal structures and information-sharing processes that discourage self-directed action. When access to information is restricted or manipulated, then the work group is not fully empowered. Even if inclined to do so, work groups hampered in their efforts to make decisions and control the factors of their own production will act reluctantly. People left in the shadows quickly recognize the powerlessness of their position and instinctively act with caution. As a leader or manager, make sure this does not happen. Barriers to empowerment and mutual participation are the following:

- Lack of a clear focus or direction
- Creating plans that are self-serving and undermine proposed goals
- Requests without explanation
- Questioning without listening
- Saying one thing and then doing another
- Making decisions that are detached from solid information or facts
- Increasing responsibility without granting corresponding authority
- Demanding changes without providing sufficient resources
- Not providing a method of recourse for injustice
- Not sharing the rewards with those who helped produce results

Group and Organizational Dynamics

Since the footing for organizational endeavor is human resources, then the conditions in which individuals perform also determine how people will behave. As indicated, the group setting in which individuals find themselves can have a huge influence on effort and productivity. A famous series of studies done at the Hawthorne plant (Cicero, Illinois) of the Western Electric Company between 1924 and 1930 found that changes in the physical environment can greatly influence group productivity and in turn group attachment—the willingness of members to cooperate and work together. The research also found that when work was considered unrewarding, associations with coworkers made the doldrums of work life more appealing and provided a means for approval, cooperation, and mutual protection. Accordingly, it was concluded that group influences rather than management pressure mostly determined the work group's response and willingness to perform or not perform.

This study and others indicate that when work is structured in a manner that facilitates group interaction and cooperation, both morale and productivity will be increased. In contrast, a major source of worker dissatisfaction is the disruption of social interactions, particularly the inability to casually discuss and share ideas about workplace issues, improvements, or changes to routine. In addition, when management creates barriers to social interaction, there is a tendency toward worker frustration. This can result in the formation of group norms that operate in opposition to organizational goals. On the other hand, when group interaction is purposefully organized toward teamwork, including problem solving and goal setting, noticeably better performance is achieved.

The organizational setting is occupied by two types of work groups. There are formal groups (those that are officially recognized by management) and informal groups (those that arise spontaneously without management intervention). Both groups operate simultaneously and exert peer pressures that have a decided impact on performance. People in these groups identify with the membership and show a great deal of loyalty to attitudes and behaviors held in common.

Formal networks are typically defined by the organizational chart. These relationships are considered the official arrangement for getting work done. Formal networks identify legitimate decision-making structures. These configurations are deliberately created by an organization's management and have a prescribed hierarchy. Although these associations are viewed by management as the right way for supervising labor and distributing resources, this might not be the reality. A workforce will often create alternate configurations when official work arrangements are poorly defined or supervision is overbearing. These informal structures operate in parallel with formal structures and are no less important.

Informal groups are found in situations where people interact on a regular basis. These relationships can be complex because roles and expected behaviors are not documented.

The job of getting work done is usually resolved through trial and error. Coworkers, out of need, ultimately figure out how to function together. Over time, these improvised routines become effective and operate without a lot of conflict. The informal network functions within the formal organizational structure and typically uses some of the officially prescribed routines. To outsiders and supervisors, it may appear as though the formal structure is operational. However, if the flow of resources and information is tracked, a different picture emerges.

Unofficial groups often operate in a way that befits the overall organization. In other cases, particularly if the formal system is muddled, the informal network may act in opposition to desired practice. The informal group's behavior may go undetected in this case because members have learned to maneuver skillfully within official structures. The system as a whole may be less effective and efficient, but nobody can point to a cause. Informal networks flourish for several reasons:

■ The arrangement maintains and strengthens norms and values the group holds as important.
■ The arrangement provides for the group's social satisfaction, security, and status.
■ The arrangement facilitates communication among members.
■ The arrangement mediates and resolves problems between members.

The informal network also creates informal leaders. These individuals arise through routine interaction. They are recognized as the persons who speak up at meetings, tend to offer the best suggestions, and recommend the most plausible direction for the group's actions. In many cases, alternate leaders may appear as competition to formal leadership because of their bearing and self-confidence. As a result, the formal organization may not want to admit there is a successful alternate culture.

The informal leader and group members can form extremely strong bonds because of their common struggle and the trial-and-error process that has shaped their relationships. Group members molded in this way are keenly aware of each other's needs, shortcomings, contributions, and abilities. They have learned over time how to provide mutual assistance to make things happen and get the job done with and without management's help. Many formal groups may not have this cohesive bond because formal structures and management practices have created both physical and psychological barriers. This often happens when specific individuals or cliques are given a favored status. Or, the act of simply competing against another department—at the expense of the whole organization—for resources and prestige can create an environment in which people merely work, not together, primarily for the benefit of their group. Acts of preference, discrimination, or bias pull at people's feeling about equity and justice, serving as a continual reminder that there is a class structure where some are favored while others are not, which diminishes the notion of common good and collective effort that rewards everyone.

Because work groups are such an influential force in terms of individual behavior, organizational and managerial practices need to create an organizational culture that builds and strengthens group relationships. Overall, groups are good for an organization as well as group members because these relationships exert a strong influence on individual attitudes, behaviors, and ultimately work performance. Much of what goes on in an organization is well beyond the capabilities of any single individual, so the capacity to work together is crucial to organizational success. People who can find common understanding and who know how to work in partnership are more productive and proficient than the legendary loner. The following are a few reasons why collaboration works:

- In the face of uncertainty, groups typically make better judgments than any single individual because ideas are tested and shaped through collective discussion.
- Based on research, groups are far more successful than individuals at solving complex problems because there is exposure to a multitude and diversity of ideas.
- Groups are more resolute and determined in their ability to accomplish a task because confidence and sureness are reinforced by other members.

Every leader and manager within the organization should be working to promote group effectiveness. This means understanding and then acting to influence the variables that encourage effective group behavior. Table 3.2 illustrates the group process. Groups function much like an open system (Hackman, 1987). There are organizational and human resource inputs that are transformed through group interaction into performance outputs. To a large extent, a group's ability to perform can be assessed on how well it converts inputs to outputs. In addition, the diagram illustrates how group effectiveness is influenced by the condition of inputs and the nature of the group process itself. Since inputs are the initial contributing factor for group success, examining their

Table 3.2 The Workgroup as an Open System

Inputs	Group Process	Outputs
• Organizational setting and structure • Task complexity and character • Interpersonal skills and attributes • Group norms and cohesiveness	• Group development • Interaction patterns • Decision making • Task activities • Group support activities	• Task performance • Group relations performance

influence is a good place to start. These input considerations are the basis for later group actions and can heighten or lessen group success.

Organizational Setting and Structure

Organizational setting and structure are primarily concerned with such characteristics as the physical arrangement of the work setting, the organization and structure of adjacent groups, availability and use of technology, the condition and availability of resources, and the character of supervisory and human relation practices. In general terms, the work environment must aid work-group efficiency and effectiveness, reduce unproductive competition, and allow a sufficient amount of time for group autonomy and decision making.

The physical setting should be adequate in terms of space, lighting, and the location of tools and equipment so people can do their jobs without encumbrance. In addition, the arrangement should support communication and allow group interaction that facilitates individual task efficiency. The organization and structure of surrounding work groups should support intragroup communication, collaboration, and cooperation rather than rivalry. Ideally, work groups should be organized so that the flow of outputs and inputs between groups is adjacent and local so waste as a result of movement is reduced. The tools and technology provided should be appropriate to the required job and accessible when desired. Needed resources should be on hand and available when required so waiting and downtime are reduced. Resources must be fit for use. Repairing, reworking, and adapting resources are a large drag on performance as well as work group morale. Human relations and supervisory practices, including goals, methods, and procedures, need to be clearly focused, facilitate group-level contributions, and be appropriate to work group maturity and capability.

Task Complexity and Character

This input has two components. The first deals with the work groups' capability to assess and meet the immediate demands for getting the work done. The second is concerned with the degree of task complexity—some jobs are more difficult than others. In general terms, the labor force must be able to size up the job's complexity and then organize and use the tools and resources available to get the work done.

This means that the workforce must be knowledgeable so the individuals can readily understand what must be done, agree on the approach, coordinate their effort, assess the completeness and quality of their work, and if necessary, make required adjustments. In short, group members must be capable of meeting the social and cultural demands of the work setting. In addition, work groups must be technically competent: able to read instructions, interpret drawings, operate tools and machinery, and do the tasks that produce the product or service. Worker skills must be up to job requirements. This implies that the organization must provide training, coaching, and mentoring so quantity and quality of outputs are not impaired. In other words, the job must be organized in such a way that complexity and difficulty do not overwhelm the work group's innate and learned skills.

Interpersonal Skills and Attributes

As well as being competent with tools, machinery, and technology, individuals in the workforce must be socially competent. The willingness of members to exert effort in aggregation with others is influenced by several factors. Among these are attributes that affect group membership, such as compatibility, homogeneity, status equivalence, and overall group size. Compatibility is based on people's desire to interact, feel included, receive and give affection, and exercise individual as well as joint control. Interpersonal influences that reinforce group coherence are described accordingly:

- *The desire for inclusion:* The individual is able to participate in informal group activities, is allowed to help out with formal work activities, is part of the communication network, and is a participant in decision making.
- *The desire for affection:* The individual is able to have close and personal relationships with other group members, is able to work and communicate on a friendly personal basis, is able to act in consort with others, is able to maintain a close social distance without feeling threatened, and is able to share feelings and emotions with others in the group.
- *The desire for control equality:* The individual is not easily led by others, does not feel the need to dominate, is able to weigh and balance others' influence, allows others to participate in discussions and decision making, seeks fairness and recourse for injustice, and is able to exercise individual as well as collective control over workplace issues and tasks.

Homogeneous groups contain members who have many ideals in common. Their interests, attitudes, and values are similar. This does not mean that there is no membership diversity, but preferences, responses to external group stimuli, and reactions tend to be comparable. For example, people of the same political affiliation have common preferences—they perceive and evaluate information similarly—and tend to behave in a consistent manner. This connection, although good at building a strong group bond, often creates an unwillingness to consider other points of view. Groupthink is a resulting problem, and those with differing points of view are frequently regarded with contempt.

Groups that perform well have homogeneous capabilities and heterogeneous attitudes. Members have a common basis for communicating and working together but enough divergent thinking so creativity and problem solving remain high. Groups that have a dissimilar mix of aptitudes and attitudes—where there is too much heterogeneity—have difficulty reconciling differences on many levels and are therefore less productive. The lesson seems to be that diversity is good, but group members must have enough experiences and values in common so cohesive relationships can be formed, enabling give-and-take communication. Therefore, care should be taken when selecting and creating work groups to include the right mix of characteristics.

Group Norms and Cohesiveness

Groups go through a maturation process. People who have worked together and associated with one another over a period of time are more proficient than those who have not been together for long. Newly formed groups will spend a while sorting out relationships with each other. Members need to figure out their relative rank, worth, and standing with others in the group—how behaviors and skills will mesh so the nitty-gritty job of work is done. In due time, however, individuals will build trust and develop unwritten rules to guide working relationships, establish norms, and develop a degree of cohesiveness.

Norms are standards of behavior that are followed by individual group members. These "rules of the road" help members anticipate one another's behavior and in turn act accordingly. Norms create a sense of predictability and stabilize relationships with coworkers and supervisors. When there is a high level of conformity to established norms, then the group's ability to perform is enhanced. Adherence to norms is influenced by member cohesiveness. In turn, cohesion is affected by those variables influencing homogeneity and heterogeneity. When members trust one another and recognize how to accommodate and utilize competencies and attributes others bring to the group, then cohesiveness will be high. Typically, among mature groups, in which members have an established history and have learned how to work with one another, cohesiveness will be high. However, this does not mean the group will always operate in the best interests of the organization. Organizations that have clear goals, supportive management that is able to build trust, and human resource practices that help the workforce meet changing demands will develop work groups that are performing with the best interests of the enterprise in mind. Those groups, which are respected as valued assets and treated equitably, will develop norms and a group culture that are compatible with the organization's goals and objectives.

The influence of group inputs on the process of task performance and group performance has several challenges for leadership, including how people are managed. Although work groups and their members enable organizations to accomplish the enterprise's intended purpose, performance is affected by individual attributes, group characteristics, and organizational characteristics. Both individual and group traits can be enhanced by creating organizational structures and by employing managerial practices that support positive group behaviors. This means creating a physical setting that is congruent with the needs of the job and allowing people to work unencumbered. Likewise, goals and expected outcomes must be clearly defined. The task itself should be structured so that the job is not beyond individual endurance or capability but challenging enough to make the work rewarding rather than unbearable. Those in supervision need to have an understanding of group behaviors and manage in a manner that reduces individual competition, enhances cooperation and teamwork, builds skills and competencies, and empowers group decision making. In general terms, leadership holds most of the cards and has the responsibility for the productivity and success of the groups working under its control.

In addition to the discussion of process inputs, performance can be appraised in terms of group dynamics. Crucial to high levels of work group performance is the group relations process. It is demonstrated through the effectiveness of decision making and the behavior of individual members toward each other. The results of these interactions can be observed in two ways: task performance and group relations performance. In simple terms, leadership and accompanying supervision can assess the effectiveness of group interactions by deciding whether work is getting done as planned and whether the work group is behaving as expected. If not, then there are fundamental group dynamics that can be influenced and ultimately changed. The group process activities that indicate effectiveness are (1) development, (2) interaction patterns, (3) communication, (4) decision making, (5) task accomplishment, and (6) support. Let us examine them in more detail.

Group Development

As indicated in the previous section, groups go through a maturation process (four conversion stages) as members gain skill and confidence in a new or unfamiliar situation. Knowing where a work group stands in its development can provide clues about its ability to perform. Ideally, high-performing personnel should be approaching the last development stage. However, if some individuals are still stuck at one of the earlier stages, then additional training and team building will be required to help them find their footing in the work environment. Table 3.3 describes behaviors that can be used to assess how people are acclimating to circumstances in a work setting. It is an adaptation of the group development model (Tuckman, 1965; Heinen and Jacobson, 1976).

As a leader or manager, try to judge work group maturity by the behaviors displayed. If the work group is still not fully committed, then use coaching, mentoring, and training in

Table 3.3 Group Development When Exposed to New Demands

Stages	Group Development Behaviors
Indifference: People are still trying to play by the old rules, or the group has been newly formed. The group is immature.	• Struggle to define task requirements and work methods • Unable to accept or establish new group norms and values • Have difficulty setting up interaction patterns and maintaining relationships • Grapple with types of decision making • Individuals try to figure out how they fit in the group
Opposition: Old habits and new structures clash as members try to establish new positions in the old pecking order or members are trying to establish a new pecking order.	• Arguments over work goals and methods • Disagreements regarding what is and what is not acceptable behavior • Competition between members and defensiveness over roles • Disagreements about how decisions should be made—individually or through a group process • Many questions about the wisdom of the actions chosen
Consideration: The work group begins to figure out how the individuals are going to work together in the new environment. The group is becoming a competent and coordinated work unit.	• More likely to agree on work goals and methods than disagree • A sense of trust and cohesiveness begins to build • Some confidence in each other's ability to perform as required • More interactions that are friendly and some sharing of personal problems • Able to reach decisions using several methods without a lot of quibbling • Belief that the solution selected might work

Table 3.3 (continued) Group Development When Exposed to New Demands

Stages	Group Development Behaviors
Cooperation: The work group displays maturity and is able to function as a skillful and fully accomplished team. Members are a cohesive unit with established norms.	• Have the ability to complete work tasks on time and at required level of quality • Work well together, are friendly, and have a common ethic about how to treat one another • Understand each other's strengths and weakness and use them to the group's advantage • Close attachment to other members • A variety of decision-making methods used • Have the ability to work through group and task problems without outside help

Source: Schultz, J.R. (2011). *Making it all work: A pocket guide to sustain improvement and anchor change.* New York: Routledge.

group behavior methods to advance the capability of those in the group. Work groups should be able to manage their own work, make decisions, solve problems, and set goals before they are considered mature and fully capable.

Group Interaction Patterns

The group interaction patterns are the degree to which members are able to function together and remain committed to organizational goals and group activities. Some groups have a particular closeness and a common attitude about how work will be done. Others do not seem to be able to organize themselves. The following are factors that define group interaction and cohesiveness:

■ *Group goals:* There is agreement on the purpose and direction of group actions. Members are able to focus activities and effort on meeting required objectives without a lot of struggle or disagreement.

- *Interaction frequency:* Group members communicate and cooperate frequently to accomplish work tasks. Individuals meet formally and informally to resolve work and personal problems so group outputs stay at desired levels.
- *Personal connection:* Members are able to form sincere, trusting, and supportive relationships. These personal relationships help group members make decisions and solve problems, which helps overcome obstacles to personal development and goal realization.
- *Competition:* The extent of disagreement within the group over roles, position, or resources should be minimal. Members must be able to pool their talents to take advantage of each other's strengths. However, some members may view those outside their group as rivals for resources and recognition.
- *Recognition:* Members are able to acknowledge and celebrate outstanding individual and group performance. The group will strive together to receive favorable evaluation from supervisors and upper managers.

Because group cohesiveness is crucial to performance ability, care should be taken to foster and reinforce activities or behaviors that encourage team building. If a group is showing low cohesiveness, it may mean there is disagreement on goals or task requirements, a mismatch in skills, or the addition of new members who do not understand group norms and lack the same level of maturity. Start by keeping everyone focused on overall organizational goals. In addition, provide the work group training in group methods that will improve their problem-solving and decision-making capabilities. Also, upgrading the group's meeting management skills and group communication skills can be useful. And, in some cases, the group's membership may need to be changed for a better mix of skills and personality attributes.

Group Communication

A work group capable of high performance is one that displays interdependency. Members interact and communicate regularly in their day-to-day activities. Extensive interactions and communications are evenly distributed. No single member dominates decision making or acts as a gatekeeper for the allocation of information.

Decentralized communication—interactions in which many group members share information—works best in most situations but is particularly valuable when activities around task performance become complex. Open communication should be valued and not subdued. However, there are always forces at work that can split a group over issues, in turn creating antagonism and differences about group direction. Silence and bickering are indicators that a work group is having difficulty adapting to the new situation.

The goal is to maintain a high level of participation and transference of information. If work group performance is below expectations, look at group interaction and communication patterns for signs of dominance by a single member or subgroup. This may be an indication of larger group problems, such as immaturity in development—members do not have enough history with one another to build cohesiveness. In any case, be willing to change the situation and intervene through problem solving. Apply training, coaching, and team-building methods that will refocus the group and advance both their team skills and work competencies. Make individual members and the work group responsible for their own work efforts.

Group Decision Making

A primary group activity is decision making. It is the process of choosing among alternative courses of action. The work group's ability to discuss and agree on a particular method for making decisions is an important indicator of growth and movement toward the mature stage of cooperation. There are several ways that decisions can be handled. A work group that is well adjusted should be able to use several different methods, depending on the situation encountered. The following summarizes decision methods that can be used when trying to reach an agreement (Schermerhorn, Hunt, and Osborn, 1988):

- *Decision by authority:* A single individual in a position of power decides what will be done. This happens without discussion by the group and direction may be based on little more than intuition and hunch. However, the group is expected to accept the decision and follow. Often, dominators will try to force decisions to enhance their power position over the group.
- *Decision by authority after discussion:* Here, a team leader, chairperson, or supervisor makes the final choice after receiving input and listening to discussion from the group. The quality of the decision is usually based on the evidence and the merit of arguments presented.
- *Decision by an expert:* The group defers its decision to a specialist who may be more knowledgeable about a particular problem and alternate methods for resolution; this is often accompanied by a group discussion and agreement with the expert's opinion.
- *Decision by subgroup:* A subgroup is given authority to study alternatives and make an appropriate choice for the larger group. Typically, the subgroup reports its intentions before acting on the group's behalf.
- *Decision by minority:* A small group is able to dominate the discussion and force its decision on the larger group; this is often done when other group members lack interest or knowledge or are absent.
- *Decision by majority rule:* The group agrees to poll members and abide by a majority vote. There is usually discussion and a presentation of arguments. However, the

decision can leave a disgruntled minority that may prove to be disquieting later.

■ *Decision by consensus:* The group continues to discuss issues and redefine solutions so terms are agreeable to everyone. This requires time and a commitment by group members to listen and have a dialogue. Often, the outcome can be viewed as less than optimal, but all agree to support the effort and are able to proceed jointly.

A mature and performing group is able to recognize the limits and value of each of these methods and uses them as appropriate. Members are not locked into a particular method or dominated by a single individual or small clique. Group performance is considered satisfactory when members are able to focus on and contribute directly to task activities. The group is able to define and solve problems that relate to work completion. In addition, they are able to strengthen and support group relationships that help enhance satisfaction. This in turn makes the group more effective and productive.

Group Task Accomplishment

A well-functioning group is able to get the job done in a timely and acceptable manner without too much discord. The way to gauge an acceptable shift in this dimension is the group's capacity to handle tasks of varying and increasing complexity. A group confronted with increasing task complexity should be able to achieve both quality and quantity requirements. Group members demonstrate this capacity to manage their common effort and reach expected results when output is driven by self-determination.

Usually, individual satisfaction is boosted as the group's ability to complete complex tasks increases. This happens because members possess suitable skills and have overcome doubt about the value of organizational goals. If task accomplishment is a problem, it probably means that some people are still unsure or uneasy about the task's complexity or technical demands. First, make sure training was sufficient so skill competency matches task demands. Next, look at group social issues. Are members willing to make a personal investment in the required task and its outcomes? Can members agree on the means for bringing a task to conclusion? In these situations, management may have to reconcile individual differences and orient members toward task completion objectives. In general, however, the work group should be able to cooperate and distribute its efforts toward the common goal of getting the job done. When the technical dimensions of the task are well balanced against group members' maturity and capabilities, then performance will be high, along with satisfaction, which reinforces motivation and the willingness to maintain sustained levels of output.

Group Support

A well-functioning and effective group has sorted out individual member roles. Everyone understands how capabilities mesh and who the informal leader is. Members are able to focus on objectives and contribute to the group's overall productive purpose. These include the ability to define and solve problems related to task accomplishment. In addition, members are able to support and maintain the group's social relationships and emotional well-being. People care about one another and watch each other's back so there are no surprises or unjustified recriminations by outsiders.

Group roles fall into two categories—task and maintenance—and are usually distributed among the members. Effective groups do a good job of managing these functions themselves. However, management should understand these responsibilities and be able to step in and assist with role-defining activities so that group performance remains

Table 3.4 Task and Maintenance Characteristics

Task	Maintenance
Information seeking: Looks to other members for information or ideas. Clarifies suggestions in terms of accuracy or seeks relevant facts. **Initiating:** Offers suggestions or brings new ideas, methods, or ways of defining a problem to the group for consideration. **Information giving:** Provides expert advice, information, and facts. Can direct the group to sources for assistance and resources. **Clarifying:** Able to coordinate member activities by clarifying relationships and the relevance of various suggestions and information presented to the group. **Summarizing:** Can focus group activities by defining key issues and underlying themes. Able to organize and order complex issues so they make sense.	**Goal setting:** Able to establish plausible goals or set a reasonable standard that the group can follow when trying to work through problems or achieve goals. **Encouraging:** Can rally the group through praise, the quest for higher ideals, or the acceptance of ideas that build solidarity. **Harmonizing:** Seeks opportunities for compromise, mediates squabbles, and helps reconcile differences of opinion. **Gate keeping:** Able to stop some members from dominating discussions and decision making so others are encouraged to participate. **Following:** Knows when to go along with group decisions and encourages other members to compromise. Helps bring closure to discussions and encourages joint group action.

high even when maturity factors are in flux. Table 3.4 summarizes these task and maintenance role characteristics.

Conflict, Competition, and Cooperation

Conflict and competition are facts of organizational life. They can lead to dysfunctional as well as functional outcomes in some instances. Conflict can produce the desire for changes that will improve operations to the benefit of customers, shareholders, and employees. And, if managed effectively, it can produce cooperation—a healthy tension between individuals so the work group or department does not fall into complacent and self-righteous routines that can lead to ineffective thinking. Competition on the other hand, although often commended as a way to improve productivity, has the opposite effect. It sets up win-lose conditions where one group is exiled to a reduced status thus frustrating any hope of future cooperation.

Conflict arises when there is disagreement over how decisions will be made, how resources will be distributed and consumed, or how work will be accomplished. The interdependence of job activities and diversity in values or perceptions can pit individuals against each other. Out of frustration, one group may try to prevail over the other by enforcing its point of view. The following are typical sources of organizational conflict:

■ *Shared resources:* There is recognition that money, materials, equipment, and space are not unlimited but must be budgeted and allocated. Departments will try to defend their needs over those of other work units.

■ *Differences in goals:* The specialization of organizational work units produces differing expectations and outcomes for each department. Units often try to maximize their output without consideration for others or at the expense of others.

■ *Interdependence of work:* The completion of work by individuals and departments is usually dependent on the output or information from many others in the organization. Depending on the degree of competition or cooperation, productivity can be reduced or enhanced by the flow of information and resources.

■ *Organizational ambiguities:* Poorly defined job responsibilities and unclear roles that result in overlap or a gap

in performance are a trigger for conflict. Poor communication or the lack of accurate information that produces
mistakes or missed opportunities will result in conflict.

▪ *Differences in perceptions or values:* The distinction in
goals and expectations for various organizational units
also produces differences in perception, attitudes, and values that can lead to conflict. For example, delivery promises made by sales may not be realistic for production.
Labor and management may differ over issues of control
and what constitutes an honest day's work.

▪ *Individual style:* Individual differences in personality and
behavior can lead to harassment, arguments, and retaliation. Authoritarian personalities or low self-esteem can
produce individual striving that angers colleagues, and
results in reprisal.

These sources of aggravation usually arise because organizational structures are not defined and clearly understood or
management within a company is not functioning as a coherent and enabling team. Such circumstances are called antecedent conditions. In other words, muddled work situations
are the breeding ground for dispute and struggle that can
bring on conflicts. Since the uncertainty created by conflicting
assignments is the starting point for conflict, work structures
and relationships should include purposely designed practices
that reduce uncertainty. This means developing a system in
which there is clarity about goals, values, means, and methods.
People are more likely to operate in a cooperative manner if
overlaps in responsibility and authority are reduced and limits for accountability understood. By being preemptive and
designing clear-cut work structures, conflict can be buffered
and often reduced.

As the leader responsible for overseeing the management
and coordination of organizational systems, recognize that
interpersonal relationships are not always neat, polite, or logical. Consequently, however, there is often a well-intentioned

effort to harmonize all work interactions. Managers trying to maintain control may be tempted to tightly define working assignments—standardize routines and describe or supervise work activities in minute detail. However, being too prescriptive can create rigidity where freedom to act when necessary can be restrained and rendered ineffective. So, caution is advised to define only those structures and related procedures that are critical to coherent operations. Allow customary and humdrum activities to adjust and accommodate prevailing needs and conditions. Manage only what is important.

Conflict can also occur if role expectations are misunderstood. An individual or individuals may not be clear about what actions should be taken to do a job well. Sometimes, the uncertainty surfaces because supervision is lacking or unclear about expectations, or the people involved lack understanding (did not listen or comprehend what had been communicated). In other cases, there may be too many demands for the time available. People are overloaded or positions understaffed, so frustration and anxiety grip the workforce, slowing progress as members grapple with the pressure. Often, managers and supervisors issue orders and make demands without allowing or encouraging feedback, questions, or requests for clarification that might build a case for assistance or an altered approach. Hoping for the best and trying to avoid blame, people will typically keep their mouths shut and push on in an uncertain and poorly coordinated manner. These role ambiguities are defined as follows:

■ *Within an individual:* This occurs when there is uncertainty about task requirements. The behavior is evident when work load interferes with other requests, when time conflicts create an overload, or when demands are beyond a person's capacity. These contradictory pressures can be unsettling and reduce individual effectiveness.

- *Between individuals:* This usually erupts because of differences in opinion or over the differential in roles (status in the hierarchy), but is more likely due to disparity in values or perception about how to manage and coordinate individual work activities. Work requirements and individual values are in conflict with another's expectations.
- *Between individuals and the work group:* Often, this is related to work group pressure requiring conformity with specific norms or accepted practices, for example, being criticized for falling behind or exceeding production goals.
- *Between work groups:* This can be caused by labor–management disagreements, but is typically due to squabbles over scarce resources. Also, tensions can be raised when one group perceives that the other is receiving more attention that is favorable.

Traditionally, supervisors were expected to deal with conflict by trying to change behavior. However, this is difficult because core feelings are closely held—part of an individual's nature—and changing them requires specific skills beyond the capability of most managers and first-line supervisors. It is far better to view conflict as normal and inevitable. This viewpoint does not require elimination or resolution, but instead acknowledges that conflict can be managed. From a workplace perspective, there are methods that can be used to reduce and in some cases eliminate conflict. Most, however, tend to suppress the underlying issues, allowing time to complete the task at hand, but may require later intervention. The following discussion on conflict reduction and resolution methods is an interpretation of ideas articulated by Thomas (1976):

- *Avoidance or withdrawal:* Pretending that the conflict does not exist. Parties withdraw from the situation in the hope that it will go away. The management technique is to tell involved individuals that circumstances do not merit a dispute and instead refocus attention on work matters, such as meeting production and quality objectives.

■ *Dominating or forcing:* When a formal authority simply dictates the solution and decides what will be gained or lost by each party. The person in authority simply says, "Cut it out," then dictates how conditions are going to be handled.

■ *Competition:* One side is allowed to win over the other through superior skill or other advantage. Supervision allows the drama to play out or assists one side and suppresses the other by controlling resources and access to information. This is typically done without the knowledge of the involved parties but can produce an identifiable inequity and attempts at retaliation.

■ *Majority rule:* Simply placing an issue on the table for a vote with the understanding that the side with the most votes has the winning position and the others must go along.

■ *Accommodating or smoothing:* The difference between disputing parties is played down, and connections or common interests are highlighted. This is where the person in charge uses diplomacy to minimize the extent and importance of disagreement and tries to convince one side or the other to give in.

■ *Negotiation or compromise:* Each party gives up something of value to the other. Both groups agree to discuss the issue, usually with the help of a facilitator or arbitrator, to decide what will be sacrificed and how future responsibilities and conditions will be carried out.

■ *Problem solving:* Both parties agree to search for a solution that everyone will accept. All involved work toward a common goal where there is a free exchange of ideas and a solution is found by weighing facts and deciding on methods for future action.

Each of these methods has advantages and disadvantages. Their use and application are dependent on the particular

Table 3.5 Conflict Reduction Outcomes

Outcome	Conflict Reduction Methods
Win-win: Conflict is managed by finding the underlying cause of issues to reconcile differences.	• Problem solving
Win-lose: One party achieves its needs at the expense and exclusion of the other party.	• Dominating or forcing • Competition • Majority rule
Lose-lose: No single party achieves its needs and underlying causes remain unsettled.	• Avoidance or withdrawal • Accommodation or smoothing • Negotiation or compromise

situation and the time available to deal with issues. Although time is often a consideration, conflict reduction methods that set up a win-lose result may need attention later. Table 3.5 organizes conflict reduction methods according to their potential outcomes.

To manage conflict effectively, those in management and supervisory roles should understand that conflict is the result of poorly defined roles, scarcity of resources, inequitable treatment, or just plain misunderstanding. Conflict is inevitable when people interact; however, it can and should be managed so quality and productivity do not become compromised. Good communication skills—the ability to listen and speak clearly—are probably the first consideration when trying to prevent disagreement. Although there are several ways to manage conflict, problem solving (people can work together at resolving issues) is the only method that creates a win-win resolution. Other methods, although effective in the short run, can have consequences that will require attention later. In the long run, however, controlling organizational structures that ensure clear goals, organize work and proportion roles, create fair and equitable practices, and allocate sufficient resources will go a long way toward reducing variables that produce conflict.

Another characteristic of organizational life that some individuals feel is an instinctive part of human nature is competition. Its drivers and attributes are similar in nature to those that are encountered when dealing with conflict. Competition is often viewed as the common underpinning of American enterprise. However, because it produces struggle that creates winners and losers, the outcomes are tenuous at best. The winners feel really good, but the losers will eventually get even—a recipe for inevitable conflict and fallout that will produce waste and loss for the enterprise.

Competition in an organizational setting can be found in two places. There is competition between group members and between various work groups. In each case, people are contending for status, resources, recognition, and rewards. In doing so, the striving creates an interesting dynamic by which loyalty and cohesion are built, but others are viewed with hostility and as the enemy. Although people are energized, the organization will suffer in the long run due to the following consequences (Daft, 1983):

- *Poor coordination:* The ability of work units and departments to work together toward organizational goals may be compromised as people strive to be the top dog.
- *Task diversion:* The energy that should be focused on task completion and goal accomplishment is diverted to winning the competition.
- *Altered judgment:* Viewpoints become biased and stilted as individuals and groups stop communicating and focus on their own needs and ability to win.
- *Loss of commitment:* Individuals and groups in the down position often lose heart, as well as feelings of loyalty or commitment to organizational goals.

Competition, although exalted by many as a stimulating force, is a double-edged sword that places large numbers of people in a second-place position. It dooms capable individuals to a reduced status where they are less likely to cooperate and participate and often become dependents of those who have taken the prize. No organization, or any enterprise for that matter, can afford to have portions of the population not fully contributing to make the prevailing environment a better place. Winning in the short run can have long-term consequences: Resentment and reduced productivity create even larger losses in the future. Competition is a losing strategy that can create organizational situations that are difficult to manage because workers are disenfranchised, uncooperative, unwilling, and dependent (take a lot of support and prompting) rather than being self-sufficient and useful. Kohn (1992) in his book, *No Contest: The Case Against Competition,* put it this way:

> Competition by its very nature damages relationships. Its nature, remember, is mutually exclusive goal attainment, which means that competitors' interests are inherently opposed. I succeed if you fail, and vice versa, so my objective is to do everything to trip you up. This attitude does not reflect a neurotic or sadistic orientation on my part. It is the heart of competition itself because competition decrees that both of us cannot succeed. (p. 132)

In general, there are two ways to manage competition in an organizational setting. One method is preventive and the other palliative. Both include strategies that focus on cooperation rather than opportunistic one-upmanship.

Prevention: Actions that can keep individuals and groups from competing against one another.
- ■ First and foremost, avoid setting up an environment in which there are win-lose conditions: People feel they must compete for resources and recognition. Build a culture where mutual sharing for the benefit of the organization and its customers is the accepted behavior.

■ Build open communication networks with unrestricted access to information, and groups can freely solicit and exchange data, ideas, knowledge, and news.

■ Encourage groups and individuals to interact as part of their daily work routine. Allow and support mutual goal-setting, problem-solving, and improvement activities. Acknowledge and support group actions that help one another.

■ Structure the work setting so process input and output flows are adjacent and not isolated from one another by department boundaries.

■ Allow and encourage people to rotate among various work groups and become proficient at several jobs.

■ Create an orientation by which people develop sensitivity toward others' diversity, understandings, and work accomplishments. Acknowledge contributions to the overall organization and not individual or group achievements.

■ Build trust. Avoid developing structures in which individuals or groups have unequal power. Create mechanisms that will allow people recourse for perceived injustices.

Palliative action: Tactics that can smooth the negative consequences of competition.

■ Use management's authority to define how competing parties will behave and operate in this particular instance. Management decides how disputed issues will be resolved and recompense distributed. Remember, however, this lose-lose solution sets up a situation that will need to be settled more equitably at some future point.

■ Play down the disputed areas of contention. Look for common interests that will focus the parties involved on organizational goals that benefit customers and stakeholders. Appeal to the common good.

- Bring disputing groups into a setting where issues can be negotiated. Facilitate an interaction in which both parties give up a portion of their resources, power, or gain so the whole organization can succeed.
- Train arguing parties in problem-solving techniques, have people work collectively on a solution that is mutually beneficial, and then allow them to implement the proposed solution jointly.

Cooperation is the antidote to potentially destructive competition. People who have learned to collaborate and work together as colleagues quickly recognize their productive capabilities. Research has shown that working together to attain common goals produces higher achievement and greater productivity. Models might be research teams, problem-solving teams, work teams, and athletic teams. This country was at its best and most productive during World War II and the postwar period when cooperation and shared sacrifice were the norm. People at all levels worked together for the common good. Cooperation means that the success of each individual is linked to that of other members in the group or society. Since most of us have worked in situations where mutual assistance and cooperation were the routine, certainly the benefits of common effort can be recognized and appreciated. Building a workplace that has at its core cooperative strategies results in one that will be a more productive and rewarding place to work.

Lessons Learned

It is hoped the discussion in this chapter provided some insights into human nature and addressed the question of why people behave as they do. There are many influences, but these can be divided into two categories: individual and situational. Individual attributes are shaped by a series of life experiences and are individually held but not easily changed—particularly by managers and supervisors. Situational factors, on the other hand, are affected by environmental conditions that can be manipulated or fashioned to create both positive and negative influences that will have a direct impact on individual satisfaction and productivity.

The following situational and environmental factors, to a large extent, are malleable. Improvement or changes in these work-setting characteristics can help eliminate job dissatisfaction. And, in some cases, particularly when policies enhance opportunity and growth, job satisfaction will be increased.

Organizational policy and conditions: The issues here are primarily structural but help determine the organization's culture. Of concern are the physical arrangement of the work setting, the organization and structure of work groups, availability and use of technology, the condition and availability of resources, and communication networks. Other factors would be attendance rules, grievance procedures, and safety considerations. Also included would be policies and procedures that encourage teamwork, cooperation, and decision making and facilitate enough self-sufficiency so work is done without extensive oversight.

Supervision: The considerations in this case are human relations issues. Of concern would be management philosophy. Are people considered an asset capable of self-direction and self-control in the pursuit of goals and work objectives? Is supervision technically and emotionally competent? Do managers provide more than direction? Are they capable of coaching and mentoring to improve job performance?

Coworker and peer relationships: Important aspects would be interpersonal relationships and group dynamics. Do people work well together? Are relationships relatively friendly, with group interactions cohesive, yet accommodating to other work units? Is communication and decision making decentralized, open, and not dominated by a few individuals?

Task structure: The primary concern is job design. Are the arrangement of tasks and the setting in which work is performed suitable to the workforce's capabilities? Do work conditions provide enough direction yet allow sufficient variety and autonomy to make the job interesting and challenging?

Skill requirements: The defining elements in this category are physical and mental: dexterity, flexibility, lifting capability, experience, and knowledge. Is the selection and hiring process discrete enough to provide the right match of capabilities suitable to work requirements? Are training and retraining programs sufficient and robust enough to orient new employees and continually upgrade skills of existing work groups?

Compensation system: The issues here are wages and benefits. How do salary and benefit packages compare to local as well as industry standards? What fraction of benefits is supported by the organization in comparison to that supported by the workforce? Can vacations or time off be scheduled and taken? Is a portion of an individual's compensation contingent on the organization's overall performance?

Opportunity and growth: These factors are supported by organizational policy and include performance appraisal methods, advancement, and the prospect to achieve and grow. These items relate to how individuals actually do their work. Does management construct systems that create opportunities for people to experience responsibility, achievement, recognition, and advancement?

The goal, of course, in trying to define and understand human nature would be efficient and effective operations that provide high-quality products and services. These are achieved by building an organization that is capable of high levels of performance. Since the workforce, the people within the enterprise, creates possibilities and gets the work done, management policies and traditions are a major consideration when dealing with behaviors that affect organizational outcomes. Substantial evidence (Pfeffer, 1998) indicates that effective management practices can produce significant economic performance. So, in resounding terms, the seven factors previously discussed must be managed in a way that engenders fulfillment—a feeling of satisfaction and pride in accomplishment. As Deming (1986, p. 77) often said, "It's the job of management to remove barriers that rob people of their pride of workmanship."

All of these situational factors are controlled by management. It is leadership's responsibility to assess and ensure that situational factors or conditions are comfortable and value centered so that people find the work setting an enjoyable yet challenging place where expectations can be realized. Organizational conditions that produce feelings of well-being and achievement are major drivers of performance. Compensation and rewards, on the other hand, are not powerful inducements that will achieve sustained outstanding performance. Sending the right signals can be the defining point in getting the workforce to create an environment that is focused on making things happen and getting work done in a way that builds strong loyalties. Consider instituting some of the following practices as a way of getting the message across:

- Define the leadership role as the conscience of organizational integrity and values. Communicate and reinforce clear values and performance standards.
- Include agenda items in executive meetings that deal with organizational performance as well as financial performance. Review organizational health, capability, and progress toward improved organizational performance.

- Organize reporting relationships so that management is seen as support for achieving organizational goals and high levels of organizational performance. Reduce the perception of a "boss-centered" organization.
- Employ and promote individuals who demonstrate management and leadership skills that reinforce ethical values, empowerment, innovation, safety, organizational learning, and high performance expectations.
- Reduce status differentiation, including office arrangements, parking, dress, and perks. Create an environment that exemplifies equity and integrity: high moral principles and professional standards.
- Communicate and share financial and performance information throughout the organization so people know and understand what is happening. Make sure groups and individuals have the information they need for decision making and problem solving.

Chapter 4

Understand How People Learn, Develop, and Improve

Introduction

Leadership, among its several competencies, is about learning—not only personal learning but also organizational learning. Thus, the primary direction for any learning organization involves creating an environment that encourages continual assessment, improvement, and renewal. The organization's long-term survival is grounded on its ability to learn and grow. This happens when individuals within the workforce are able to improve their capabilities and skills so they can solve problems, make decisions, and contribute to the organization's well-being. According to W. Edwards Deming (1986, p. 86), "No organization can survive with just good people. They need people who are improving." No organization can prosper for long in a global economy without people who are capable and adaptable and know how to learn.

This chapter examines how people learn, develop, and improve. The topics covered are as follows:

■ Learning is about theory
■ Organizational learning
■ Learners are not all alike
■ Growth comes from lessons learned
■ Reinforcing and sustaining learning

Learning Is about Theory

Learning is acquired knowledge that is built on theory. Theory, in turn, leads to a prediction—that is hopefully right— about future outcomes when new ideas are put into practice. Learning is the continual interplay between theory (ideas) and application (experience) producing an adaptive response in the form of knowledge. Knowledge in this case usually means gathering information, and more importantly, understanding what the information means—its implications—and then being able to translate that appreciation into useful action. Too often, people respond to information without first realizing what is inferred or what the resulting action will bring. An instinctive rush to conclusion occurs without consideration, which usu- ally creates additional problems that require resolution later. Organizations are full of individuals who are well versed, can sell the merchandise, keep the books, order the materi- als, and push the product out the door, yet the mistakes these informed people make can ultimately drive a company into the ground. The automotive industry and other old-line manu- facturers who have lost market share in the current economy are examples of the attrition that has taken place in many industrial sectors because leaders and managers did not learn, did not ascertain and understand the results of their actions.

Learning takes place when an observation about events produces a question. In response, the information gathered is tested and examined against other opinions and insights, then shaped by outcomes (experiences) and applied in a continual cycle that allows further investigation and renewal. Therefore, as Deming (1994, p. 103) has implied, learning is acquired knowledge that is built on theory. Theory in turn leads to a prediction—with the risk of being wrong—about future outcomes when the new practice is applied. Accordingly, he concludes:

> It is the extension of application that discloses inadequacy of theory, and the need for revision, or even a new theory. Again, without theory, there is nothing to revise. Without theory, experience has no meaning. Without theory, one has no questions to ask. Hence without theory, there is no learning.

Subsequently, being informed or well trained does not mean something was learned. Learning takes place when the interaction with current circumstances produces a need to move from the abstract to the concrete or from apathy to action. This need for change produces a hunch, an idea, a theory about what can be done, which leads to the search for knowledge and the application of the new understanding as an answer or acquired skill. Learning is the continual interplay between theory or training and an adaptive response to a particular experience. Figure 4.1 illustrates these relationships.

Leadership is largely about prediction. Leaders and managers are responsible for moving the organization in a direction that will benefit customers, stakeholders, and other constituencies. This process of setting and communicating direction is really a theory—a hunch based on information gathered from the surrounding environment. The information contains numerical data, observations, and judgment grounded in experience. This synthesized guess about the future is put into a plan and then tested through application against an idealized model about what will happen. As actions are rolled out and exposed to the real world, adjustments are made to

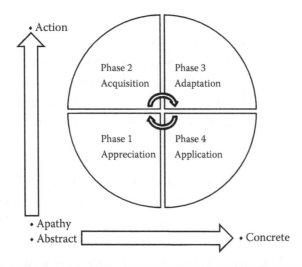

Figure 4.1 Cycle of learning.

accommodate prevailing realities. There is a continual inter-play between ideas and actual events. If there is learning, an understanding based on knowledge, then the organization will survive and even thrive. Learning is a perceptive and natural process. The learning cycle contains the following four phases:

1. *Appreciation:* An interest is aroused. Questions are asked. There is recognition that the current way is not working, and something different is required. A search for answers and new ideas begins.
2. *Acquisition:* Observations are made and informa-tion is gathered. Problem solving may be employed to gain up-to-date insight about what is really occurring. Knowledge is expanded. A theory is conceived.
3. *Adaptation:* The information is processed, and a judg-ment is made about how the new capability will be integrated into the current setting as an action for change or updated skill. There is a new understanding. Individual proficiency and behavior are modified.
4. *Application:* The new idea or skill is put into practice and the results are observed. The theory is tested. If outcomes

do not meet expectation, then the cycle is repeated. Or, in many cases, expectations are met, but over time the installed method no longer meets changing needs and the cycle begins again.

Organizational Learning

The application of learning based on an observed need for change is often handled in a matter-of-fact manner. It is automatic and used with little cognitive effort. For example, when hanging a picture, driving to work, or even writing a report and preparing a budget, these activities, to some degree or another, employ the learning cycle. Life and work are filled with such activities, which are mundane but utilize a learned response. Survival, a person's existence in the world, is really a continual replay of the learning cycle. However, when generalizing these concepts to organizational learning, the linkage between appreciation and application requires a more formalized approach.

To that end, Deming preferred to employ the PDSA cycle—Plan, Do, Study, and Act. It was developed using a concept he picked up from his friend and mentor Walter Shewhart. The cycle can be applied with any recurring activity or to evaluate changes that are the result of short-term and long-term planning. The following are the stages or phases:

1. *Plan:* Based on the situation, decide what will be done. Determine the goal and how outcomes will be measured and assessed. Develop a set of actions and sequence the activities.
2. *Do:* Put the plan into action. Carry out the steps and let the process run. If the investment is large or the action complex, test on a smaller scale first.
3. *Study:* Observe the results, gather facts based on data, assess outcomes against expectations, and draw conclusions.

4. *Act:* If outcomes meet expectations, scale up and integrate into the normal routine. If outcomes are not meeting expectations, problem solve and devise a modified or new approach. Repeat the cycle.

The cycle is repetitive and ongoing. When used, it keeps people from leaping into action without first considering how changes will be handled and then anticipating results. It provides a buffer, a way of slowing and then appraising actions. It forces personal learning and helps less-experienced managers recognize that two points of data do not indicate a trend. Ideas and proposed solutions to a problem are tested, which then provides an opportunity for recovery when actions do not produce the desired result. Using the PDSA cycle reduces the inclination to operate by the seat of the pants.

More important, using PDSA encourages the measurement and analysis of outcomes. The study phase promotes the use of data to determine trends, make cause-and-effect comparisons, and verify assumptions. A resulting consideration when applying PDSA becomes the selection and use of metrics and process measurements. These reflections help uncover cause-and-effect relationships that ultimately lead to operational and fiscal improvements. The measurements selected provide a clear basis for aligning change with the organization's goals and purpose. Analysis in this context reinforces the meaning of discovery, gained from data and information, as support for decision making and conclusions. In short, outcomes are evaluated against expectations using facts. This, in turn, verifies the new approach as a better way for getting work done.

In addition, the PDSA cycle can be used to assess the personal learning cycle. The results of training are evaluated against proposed goals and outcome measurements. In this framework, personal learning and organizational learning are joined symbiotically. There is a mutual and beneficial relationship. Organizations do not typically learn and grow unless their members—while interacting with the environment or

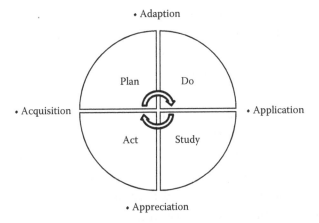

Figure 4.2 The continuous cycle of learning and improvement.

organizational processes—recognize a need or opportunity and consequently go through the four learning phases to grow personally. The ability to achieve high levels of performance requires an organizational approach that encourages and supports personal learning.

The relationship between learning and improvement as a continuous cycle is illustrated by Figure 4.2. This process is ongoing and, if applied as intended, prevents organizational rigidity, atrophy, and obsolescence. Learning and improvement are the ongoing interaction between acquisition, where information is gathered and a theory is formed, and application, where ideas are tested and evaluated.

A learning organization is one that continually seeks to improve its existing systems, processes, and tactics through adaptive changes that lead to new goals and methods. The notion of continual learning needs to be embedded in the organization's collective psyche and practiced as:

■ Knowledge sharing throughout the organization
■ Organizationally supported opportunities for personal and unit learning
■ Problem solving at the lowest possible level—at the source where issues are detected

- Part of daily work routines
- A realization that change in response to stakeholder needs and organizational possibilities is really an opportunity to learn and improve

Learning organizations create a culture in which awareness, understanding, assessment, and improvement are a matter of doing business. Thus, learning in this case is about continually testing ideas and gaining from the experience. The knowledge produced is shared and creates a capacity for further inquiry and renewal. The cycle for continuous learning is applied and reapplied using projects that demand study, reflection, collaboration, and ultimately, action. In the stories that follow are examples of organizational learning—recognizing an opportunity and then fixing it and evaluating the results.

A major teaching hospital observed that patients presenting in the emergency room with congestive heart failure often reappeared within 90 days of discharge. An aggressive program for case management was put into place that used collaborative interaction between caregiver and patient. Prior to discharge, patients participated in give-and-take discussions about medications, diet, and exercise. In addition, they were scheduled with a primary care physician for follow-up, and a case nurse was assigned to make sure the patients were following their program and keeping appointments. The new information on readmissions was compared to data from the previous two years. The results indicated a rapid decline in patients showing up a second time and an ongoing trend that was below the previous two-year average (Carey, 2003).

The state of Wisconsin over several years had provided education and counseling for drivers who accumulated 9 points against their driver's license. People who receive 12 points lose their driving privileges. Some Transportation Department employees thought the counseling services were redundant and ineffective at reducing the actions of repeat offenders. An experiment was conducted where every

10th driver was excused from the driver's counseling inter-
view. Factors such as age, gender, and previous driving
record were tracked separately to eliminate biases. After
two years, the analysis showed no significant difference
between those who received counseling along with training and those who received training only. The program was
consequentially altered to eliminate the additional driver's
consultation, saving several million dollars (Joiner, 1994).

Learners Are Not All Alike

Almost everyone recognizes that others view and perceive the
world in slightly different ways. We all gather information and
make decisions about events according to different patterns.
These patterns are part of an individual's persona and are the
result of early experiences and fundamental traits. This means
that learning experiences should have sensitivity and tolerance
toward various learning styles. Creating an optimal learning
environment starts with a more collaborative and open environment in which learning can be individualized. This is in
contrast to traditional models that have the learner sit passively
while someone with authority describes how the world works
and how activities ought to be done.

The Swiss-born psychiatrist Carl Jung (Hanson et al., 1986;
Kroeger and Thuesen, 1992) suggested learning is a two-step
process; first perceptions are made (information is collected), and
then these are judged (analyzed and mentally processed). There
are two ways of perceiving or finding out about how the world
works: sensing and intuition. Those who are sensers operate in
the here and now. Such individuals are active learners who focus
on the immediate and grasp ideas by doing. On the other hand,
intuitives have a longer perspective. These individuals prefer to
watch and observe and then reflect on what is occurring.

The two means for judging perceived information are
thinking and feeling. Thinking judgments tend to be rational.
These are based on fact, logic, and external evidence. Decision

making in this case is often impersonal. In contrast, feeling judgments are based on values, personal beliefs, and subjective internal evidence. Decision making for these individuals is based on likes and dislikes.

Jung's theory concludes that people tend to use one perception and one judgment style at a time. Depending on the situation, opposite combinations may be used, but not at the same time or with the same frequency. The preference for a particular arrangement develops over time and becomes the comfortable way for making sense of the environment. These preferences become a style for learning as well as teaching (Hanson, Silver, and Strong 1986). Jung's theory—the idea of characterizing human behavior based on two sets of opposing factors—provides a method for classifying learning that produces these four learning styles: listeners, watchers, doers, and conceptualizers.

> *Listeners:* These are people who learn through listening and conversing with others. The spoken word and specific examples are their approach to learning. As learners, they express themselves using conversation and give-and-take discussion. Taking time to reflect is important to a listener.
>
> *Watchers:* These are people who learn through visual means. Media—videos, television, and film—as well as the written word are their preference for learning. As learners, they express themselves through pictures, charts, graphs, media, written reports, and group projects. Working with others is important to a watcher.
>
> *Doers:* These are people who are hands on. Experimentation, trial-and-error efforts, and active engagement are their preferred methods of learning. As learners, they express themselves through projects and by manipulating objects in their environment. Finding an answer—something that works—is important to the doer.
>
> *Conceptualizers:* These are people who learn through logical thinking and rational evaluation. Theory and systematic analysis are the basis for their learning. As learners,

they express themselves through written reports, flow charts, and artistic composition. Discovery through simulation and activities that require logical and analytical thinking is important to the conceptualizer.

Figure 4.3 illustrates how the pairing of perception and judgment preferences result in four different learning styles. This process of considering events and rationalizing them for use has several implications. First, programs requesting organizational change and renewal will be perceived and processed in different ways by those affected. In the absence of formalized direction or instruction, people will fumble around as they grapple with issues and search for a mutually agreeable approach. Second, this period of struggle takes time and may produce unintended consequences. However, formalized training that facilitates personal and organizational learning can reduce the transition period and the possibility for mistakes. Education and training, particularly methods that accommodate an individual's preferences, will significantly increase competency transfer, facilitate collaborative inquiry, and accelerate the integration of new techniques into daily work so processes are revitalized. Creating a learning environment is crucial to an organization's growth and overall survival.

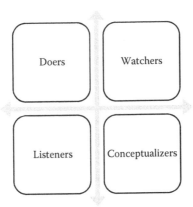

Figure 4.3   Learning styles.

Although there are differences in how people learn, adults as a group have some common tendencies when confronted with formal learning situations. The use of adult learning principles increases commitment, retention, and the ability to provide meaningful content. When developing training, content design should include features that recognize learner maturity. The following are suggestions for adapting training to adult learners (Schultz, 2008):

- Instructional materials should be situation oriented rather than content oriented or abstract.
- Accept and encourage active involvement by participants.
- Use instructional materials and activities that build on the learner's experiences.
- Create a collaborative learning environment rather than one that is authority centered.
- Solicit learner input when designing and structuring training activities.
- Assessment should have criteria mutually agreed on by the learner and instructor.
- Assessment ought to permit reappraisal and additional opportunities for improvement.
- Activities need to be experience based rather than theoretical.

Remember, when introducing system or process improvements, opportunities for learning that consider individual differences and relate new patterns to past experience are most likely to be successful. Adult workers bring considerable knowledge with them. Through trial and error, they have developed operable structures for getting work done in the current situation. Do not shortchange their efforts and capabilities when fashioning new work arrangements. Respect and consider work group needs and learning patterns when improving operations. Table 4.1 describes adult learner characteristics.

Table 4.1 Adult Learner Characteristics

Learner Characteristics	Learner Implications
Self-concept: Adult learners see themselves as capable of self-direction and desire others to see them in the same way. A capacity for self-direction is the way adults define maturity.	A climate for openness and respect is helpful in identifying what learners want and need. Adults enjoy planning and carrying out their own learning activities. Adults need to be involved in setting and evaluating their own progress toward goals.
Experience: Adults bring life experiences to the learning process. Adults define who they are in terms of experiences. They are who they are as a result of these combined experiences.	There is less use of transmittal techniques such as lectures but more use of experiential techniques. Discovery of how to learn based on past experience is part of self-actualization. Mistakes are opportunities and part of the learning process. Discounting experience discredits the adult learning process.
Readiness to learn: Adult development is increasingly toward occupational and social competence. Seasoned and experienced individuals are eager to advance skills that prepare them for work and life.	Adults need opportunities that help identify competency requirements for social and occupational roles. Adults' readiness to learn and teachable moments occur when learning opportunities coincide with the need to know. Adults can best identify their own readiness to learn and teachable moments.

continued

Table 4.1 (continued) Adult Learner Characteristics

Learner Characteristics	Learner Implications
Time and problem orientation: Adults think and learn as a way of being more effective in their immediate environment.	Adult education needs to be problem centered rather than theoretical.
	Curriculum development should focus on what the learner needs to function in the current environment.
	Adults need opportunities to learn quickly and apply ideas promptly.

Source: Adapted from Knowles, M., 1981, *The adult learner: A neglected species.* Houston, TX: Gulf.

Growth Comes from Lessons Learned

Organizational growth and renewal typically include implementation steps that alter the flow of work and the deployment of labor to create more effective and efficient systems. New connections and relationships are established that reinforce the latest methods. Yet, often, employees are expected to function as if nothing changed. Consequently, work groups are left to their own devices and adaptive wits to accommodate novel and unfamiliar arrangements.

Regardless of how much they would like to, or how hard they try, employees cannot perform well in an altered job situation until they know what is expected and how tasks should be handled. With that end in mind, a well-developed training program should be used to ease transition efforts and address the "what" and "how" of the new work arrangement. Training or retraining should not be left to chance when alterations of any scale are put into place. There is too much at stake; momentum can be lost and improvements can founder as people try to redefine their responsibilities and relationships. Flagging resistance may also reassert its influence as frustrations rise while bewildered workers adapt to their new conditions.

Therefore, training ought to be part of any program that improves or changes organizational potential. The opportunity to learn and grow helps build confidence and reduces uncertainty about altered roles and expectations. Both workers and supervisors will appreciate the chance to improve their usefulness and expand skills so they can readily function in the reconfigured environment. However, teaching methods and styles need to accommodate learner preferences and bridge the teacher's predilections and biases. Yes, leaders, managers, and trainers are shaped and guided by their own surroundings. As individuals with influence and control over other's work environment and life circumstances, they perceive the world through their own preferences. Unfortunately, they expect others to conform to that point of view. The result is often misunderstanding, resistance, and sometimes open conflict. Personal beliefs that are viewed as the only right way can hinder the teaching–learning relationship. Typically, subjective beliefs about adult learners in an instructional setting fall into the following three categories: beliefs about purpose, beliefs about subject matter, and beliefs about teachers and teacher–learner transactions (Apps, 1989).

Beliefs about purpose: These assumptions include instruction that meets needs, helps people to learn how to learn, has social or organizational value, and transmits information. Certainly, these are all laudable goals, but do they really produce learning? The question becomes, whose needs are met? Are they the learner's, the organization's, or the instructor's requisites? Why isn't helping people learn what to learn a more preferable purpose? Why are social or organizational values more important than the individual learner's standards or beliefs? Last, maybe education should empower rather than serve as a conveyor belt for transmitting information.

Beliefs about subject matter: These assumptions assert that specific objectives and competencies are needed, that the experiences and writings of certain experts are the source of knowledge, or that the organization's method of going about its business is the only approach. Such preferences fail to consider the extent of knowledge that adult learners have as a result of their own experiences. Refusing to consider indigenous knowledge often stifles organizational learning and leaves the company vulnerable to its own incestuous thinking. New and ingenious ideas or methods are stifled or set aside while the competition eats the firm's lunch. A good example is Toyota versus General Motors. One company was recognized for cultivating worker ingenuity; the other viewed employees as a tool—a means of production.

Beliefs about teachers and the teacher–learner transaction: The assumption is that the teacher is the expert, the teacher should be in control, the teacher is the master illuminator, or the teacher provides sufficient inputs and evaluates the learner's outputs. The goal in these models, of course, is to manage people's thinking, create a controlled environment, suppress resistance, maintain order, and hope for growth. This thinking fosters the notion that teachers pour information into empty heads and hope that nothing leaks out. Unfortunately, such assumptions fail to consider the learners' inclinations and experiences. Some people learn best in groups; others learn better by themselves. Some individuals prefer lectures; others learn by watching videotapes. Hands-on manipulation may work best in other cases. The teaching and learning interaction is not about what should be done but how it is done.

Instruction, teaching, and mentoring are part of the learning process. However, the approach needs to be learner- or student-centered rather than instructor- or boss-centered. Those who are true leaders recognize that most people want to do the best they can at work, and when given the opportunity to improve, they will do so if the instructional process does not threaten their sense of worth and well-being. Using methods that try to shove knowledge down someone's throat will not produce learning and may only create fear. Education and training need to be part of an open and welcoming process that is continually accessible while aimed at the broader notion of self-improvement. Deming (1986) recognized this need in his 14 points for management. Two of the points—6 and 13— addressed this issue as an opportunity to improve and transform industry's capability. These are summarized, respectively, as institute training on the job and institute a vigorous program of education and improvement for everyone.

Institute training on the job: Everyone needs training. Management must learn about the company and act on the problems that rob workers of their ability to carry out their work with satisfaction. Workers need to know the problems of production and how to do their job better. Everyone learns in different ways. Some have difficulty with written instructions; others have difficulty with the spoken word. Some people learn best by pictures, others by imitation, and some by a combination of methods.

Institute a vigorous program of education and self-improvement for everyone: What an organization does not need is just good people; it needs good people who are continually improving. This can happen when the opportunity for knowledge is available to everyone. The concern should not be for courses of instruction that provide immediate gain, but for knowledge that has long-term benefits for the individual, the firm, and society. Those organizational behaviors that produce fear, a fear of learning, need to be driven out of the organization.

Learning in this context should provide two different opportunities for engagement. One option is organizationally sanctioned and focused toward providing knowledge or skills that the workforce will need to do their jobs better and meet changing workplace requirements. The other prospect for learning should be less focused and at the discretion of individuals or work groups. The goal in this case should be the fulfillment of immediate or long-term needs as well as personal and societal needs. In either case, the act of teaching must accommodate the learner's style preferences and sensibilities as an adult with intrinsic knowledge. This means creating an environment that is nonthreatening, comfortable, and not hierarchical—creating a place where there is collaboration, active discovery, and time for individual reflection. The practices employed should put learners at the center and allow individuals to take charge of their own learning. Instructional methods should include a variety of techniques that seek to involve participants in the learning process and reduce negative views toward learning.

Teachers and mentors who function well in this climate should be less concerned with structure and order but instead develop a tolerance toward a learning process that is free-wheeling and a bit more chaotic with collaborative activities, mutual exchange, action exercises, and case studies. The goal should be initiating the learning process and then getting out of the way. The teaching process—in which actions arouse learning—should engage the learning cycle. The model that accommodates the natural learning cycle is an adaptation of David Meier's (1995) thinking: arouse interest, engage the learner, facilitate integration, and enable application.

Arouse interest: Start by establishing a positive relationship. Do activities that raise curiosity, create a desire, awaken possibilities, raise questions, calm fears, and remove barriers. Ask the learners, the participants, to identify their goals for the training. Establish what the group already knows, what these individuals want from the process,

and what benefits they expect. Discuss with participants
and decide what outcomes and competencies should be
achieved and how results will be assessed.

Engage the learner: Learners encounter new information
or methods. Use any of the visual, auditory, and tactile
methods described in Table 4.2 to create a learning experience. Arrange for learners to have an experience or
observe an experiment, an actual event, and then have
them debrief and explain what was discovered. Have
learners read something, perform a skill, shadow a more
experienced worker, watch a video, do an exercise, solve
a problem, or complete a case study and then have them
draw conclusions and explain or show what was learned.
This process is about moving from concept to conclusion
by learning, doing, and then assessing. Use multiple
assessment methods that involve the learner. The questions should be: What happened? Why did it happen? Did
the knowledge gained meet the learners' needs?

Facilitate integration: Provide an opportunity for learners to
play with the new information or skill. Get them to try out
their new skills, gain experience through trial and error,
exercise judgment, establish meaning, draw conclusions,
and connect the new method with what is already known.
The goal, of course, is to have learners encounter the situation, play with it, reflect on it, make sense of it, relate what
was discovered to past knowledge, and then integrate the
new understanding into current skills or operations.

Enable application: The new knowledge or skill is transferred to a real-world situation. Have learners problem
solve using the new information or skill, accomplish
something meaningful, or demonstrate competency in a
work setting. If results do not meet expectations, provide
additional opportunities that allow the learner to reengage
and integrate the new concept in a slightly different manner. Do not be impatient, but try to understand what

Table 4.2 Instructional Methods

Learner Involvement	Method	Description
Learner listens or watches	Lecture	Talking and verbal imagery are used.
	Reading	Printed content, including handouts and assigned text, is used.
	Demonstration	Activities are modeled, either live or filmed.
Learner writes, talks, or responds	Programmed instruction	Information is delivered in small sequential steps using self-paced activities and responses.
	Structured discussion	Instructor leads, aiming at specific objectives, using statement-and-response format.
	Panel discussion	Expert panel delivers short lectures and involves learners in sharing ideas and opinions.
	Open discussion	Instructor serves as moderator while learners share ideas and opinions on a specific topic.
	Question-and-answer session	Instructor assigns a topic, and learners develop questions and respond with answers.
Learner manipulates or operates	Performance tryout	Under instructor direction, learner actually performs specific tasks.

Table 4.2 (continued) Instructional Methods

Learner Involvement	Method	Description
Learner makes decisions and creates knowledge products	Brainstorming	Learner is asked to develop diverse ideas around a specific issue.
	Case study	Learner is asked to develop and present a solution for a hypothetical situation.
	Incident processing	Learner is asked to analyze and problem solve a specific event.
	Task team	A small group of learners is asked to problem solve and present recommendations.
	Fishbowl	Learners are asked to observe and analyze the activities of a specific operation or another group.
	Role play	Learners are asked to assume specific behaviors, act out scenarios, and then analyze results.
	Simulation	Learner is asked to work through a real situation and then analyze results.
	Clinic	Learner is asked to confront a real-life situation and develop a method or solution.

Source: Adapted from Laird, D., 1978, *Approaches to training and development.* Quezon City, Philippines: Addison-Wesley.

was missed and what else might be needed to enable less-proficient learners so they can operate in the new environment. Celebrate a job well done when learners are able to demonstrate their capability. Be generous with praise and compliments when all goes well.

When considering and designing a learning program, use a multidimensional approach. Students often need to encounter material at different levels of involvement and more than once. Therefore, structuring learning opportunities that progress from instructor show and tell, to active learner involvement, and then to hands-on application will set and reinforce new skills at a level that makes integration more certain.

Choosing which instructional methods work best in a particular situation depends on the participant's prior knowledge, innate skills, mental attitude, level of anxiety, and time available for curriculum design and instruction. The following are questions that can help clarify the selection of instructional methods (Schultz, 2008):

1. *How complex is the information or skill that will be introduced?* More complex concepts typically require multiple approaches. These might include reading for preparation, lecture and demonstration to present the concept, discussion to understand the concept, and performance trial to master the concept.
2. *How resistant will participants be to active involvement, the use of certain technology, or passive activities like reading, listening, and watching?* Adapt the method selected to the learners' likes, dislikes, and capacity to interact. As an example, small-group activities may not work well in an environment where participants are not accustomed to teamwork and collaboration—where the basic skills for group interaction have not been taught or applied.
3. *How much time is available to secure skills or knowledge transfer?* Recognize that learning activities may take

longer than anticipated. Select methods that will allow participants to complete the full training and learning cycle. Make certain learners engage in knowledge integration and skill application, the two steps that move the learner from concept to reality and enable comprehension. In any case, do not let time pressures force the use of only passive or instructor-dominated activities. If more time is needed, take steps to ensure it is available.

4. *How confident are you in the ability to apply specific methods?* Plan for and use techniques that have worked well in past situations. However, do not limit the approach to only a few time-worn practices. Introduce and use new methods if time pressures are low and if participants will tolerate experimentation or a less-polished approach. Think in terms of facilitation, not as a lecturer or presenter, but as a learning helper, as a person who makes learning easy by getting learners involved and in charge of their own learning.

5. *How much work is involved in preparing for and using a specific method?* Consider access to equipment, room availability, and setup requirements. Developing a case study or activities for which there are high levels of team processing may not fit development time available. Think about limiting the number of activities. For example, rather than doing a case study with incident processing and brainstorming, instead use the case study coupled with a structured discussion. Be flexible and adaptable and look for methods that emphasize collaboration and mutual exchange but are not big consumers of time.

Creation of a learning environment—one in which learners are eager to learn and not anxious about being judged—is shaped by both teaching style and instructional methods. Style must take into account the adult learners' mature understanding of the world and their prior experiences. On the other hand, methods must accommodate the learners' preferences and the way they perceive and judge information. These co-contributors to learning must be nurtured and become part of the organization's value system. Without the support of leadership and senior managers who understand how people learn, develop, and improve, the workforce will not produce the lessons learned and, consequently, organizational growth. Survival will be compromised, leaving the enterprise at risk of collapse as competitive and environmental pressures challenge its ability to stay relevant or compete.

Reinforcing and Sustaining Learning

Organizational longevity is rooted in culture—the display of collective behavior. Culture is influenced by a set of shared norms and values that have developed over time. The idea of continuous improvement achieved through continuous learning is a profound organizational value. Learning—the ability to gain knowledge—therefore needs to be preserved and made an integral part of the organizational routine. Doing so means anchoring the lessons learned about how people learn, develop, and improve in the culture.

Unfortunately, culture is a powerful force that is often difficult to overcome and then alter. If, for example, the current culture is inwardly focused and more concerned about preserving methods and ideas that in the past have been successful, then the organization may not be able to respond to changing market conditions adequately. General Motors and Chrysler come to mind as organizations that had inbred cultures not capable of confronting the realities of a changing business climate and ended up being bailed out by taxpayers.

Every organization exhibits a culture. The departments and work units within the organization also have a culture. Any time people work together for an extended period, a culture is formed. It is the force that guides and directs how people will interact with one another and deal with those beyond their group or organization. The following are attributes that, when operating together, shape an enterprise's culture (Price Waterhouse, 1996):

- *Values:* These are principles considered by the group to be the right way for doing work. Values are ideals displayed during individual transactions and interactions. Collegiality and teamwork are examples.
- *Norms:* These are formal and informal rules or standards that guide how people work together and relate to others outside the group. An example might be, "People work long hours and late nights around here."
- *Beliefs:* These are mental models or assumptions that people hold to be true. Beliefs are attitudes that influence an individual's perception and control decisions and actions. Examples are, "Our company is the market leader," or "The marketing department has the final say on which new products are developed."
- *Symbols:* These are rituals and traditions that communicate what is important to the business, department, or work group. Probably most noticeable is the arrangement of office space or who eats at which tables in the lunchroom.
- *Philosophy:* This is the policies that guide employee behaviors and the viewpoints that often become embedded in employee handbooks and are made apparent by vision and mission statements. "Quality is job one" is a recognizable example.
- *Environment:* This is the system's overall feel and atmosphere. It is revealed both in physical terms like workplace amenities and in the political-social tone. Here are two examples: Management operates from behind closed doors. Since the arrival of the new company president, women are now receiving promotions.

Any part of an organization subjected to change has a culture that must be considered and managed. The work groups that operate within the organization have developed a culture. Their demeanor, how they relate to one another, and how they confront issues and resolve them are due to culture. Since culture has such a large impact on individual actions and how people accomplish work, there is an overwhelming temptation by leaders and managers to manipulate cultural attributes— values, norms, beliefs, symbols, philosophy, and environment. However, culture is created and shaped by a cascade of influences. The attributes displayed are a product of many interactions. These are organizational qualities that cannot be easily manipulated. As a leader considering how to make learning a permanent value and part of the organization's culture, do not try to reshape cultural attributes. Focus instead on those mechanisms that drive the underlying elements of attribute formation and can influence changes in the quality of attribute expression. In summary, the following are six methods that can be used to lock in those qualities that shape and create a learning organization:

1. *Frame and communicate the circumstance for making changes.* Define why organizational learning is important to individual growth and ultimately company growth. Cut through the clutter of daily influences that can create complacency so everyone understands why it is necessary to move in a new direction.
2. *Develop and communicate a strategy so people can buy in to it.* Develop a central theme, a purpose, that people can rally around and create a sense of urgency so those affected are ready to take a chance on something that is different.
3. *Display actions and behaviors that set an example.* Begin to operate in a way that shows everyone what conduct is acceptable. Actions that display contrary thinking or privileged or guarded behavior send a mixed message that cannot be easily explained away. Do not get caught

saying one thing but doing another. Be willing to reflect honestly on successes and failures.

4. *Create an infrastructure that will facilitate the new way for doing work.* Infrastructure is the framework that coordinates the division of labor, the flow of resources and communication. It is typically defined by organizational charts, flowcharts, and work instructions. Begin to put people in position who reflect and practice values that are compatible with the newly defined direction. If need be, change key people. Sometimes, turnover is what is needed.

5. *Develop people-centered methods that are helpful.* These include those practices related to hiring, employee development, promotion, discipline, and termination. Treatment must be considered as fair and compassionate in these instances. Also, consider and make sure people have the right information and support so operating within the revised work culture is not intimidating.

6. *Clarify performance standards and how outcomes will be measured.* Performance standards describe the boundaries for responsibility and authority. In addition, these standards define what is acceptable and what is not. When modifying the culture, develop processes for which expectations for results are explicitly and clearly stated.

All that being said, however, the key cultural driver is leadership. Being the leader, in any case, will not be easy. Some people at both managerial and operational levels will not want to see their way of operating upset. These individuals have gained respect and a certain level of comfort under the current arrangement. But if new ideas and the future way of operating are going to become reality, then leadership will have to make sure everyone is on board and moving in the same direction. This means building an organizational climate that is nimble and capable of changing in a fluid business environment—articulating a compelling future and championing a learning environment where people are capable of acting when new opportunities present themselves.

Learning, training, and retraining are essential to creating the skills and capacity necessary to succeed in the long run. People who are learners will be comfortable when confronting new challenges because they understand how to engage the learning cycle and apply the PDSA method to uncover workable solutions. More so than others, individuals accustomed to learning—who know how to appreciate, acquire, adapt, and apply—are open to new ideas, able to solicit information and facts, can analyze and reflect, and then can draw conclusions that have relevance for application. Leaders who understand how people learn, develop, and improve are those individuals who will survive over the long term and continue to be extremely important to the business, employees, and the community at large. A leader who understands how people learn has a powerful tool that can change organizational direction and increase the enterprise's survival in spite of environmental competition and complexity.

Chapter 5

Understand the Variability of Work

Introduction

Most people understand the world is not a neat and orderly place, that day-to-day activity is buffeted by complexity, and that success means helping others find a plausible course of action in a challenging environment. People in charge, however, often provide direction that is shaped by intuition, sometimes emotion, or far too often, comparisons that assign judgment based on the amount of negative or positive movement in financial data. Although seemingly sound, following this guidance for action can be mostly a gamble.

Holding a leadership position means having to make choices, having to decide among several courses of action. And one of the most difficult things to avoid in this case is making the wrong choice—drawing the wrong conclusion—without comprehending the true nature of the conditions involved. So, an understanding based on measurement and study, the gathering of facts, helps sort out cause-and-effect relationships and reduce the chance of moving in the wrong direction.

This chapter examines the consequences of variability—the routine irregularity of impacts—on system and process activity and then recommends some rules that can be used to assess trends and detect when a process needs attention. Encouraging action when none is required or rewarding what is perceived as a positive change and likewise questioning apparent downturns, however, can have unintended consequences. Such actions often create problems when none existed previously. This chapter is organized accordingly and covers the follow issues:

- Data provide a basis for decision making
- System ups and downs are a matter of routine
- Visualizing process variability
- The process behavior chart
- Interpreting process behavior
- Tampering can be costly
- So what?

Data Provide a Basis for Decision Making

> Whatever a manager does he does through making decisions.
>
> **Drucker, 1954, p. 352**

The importance of decisiveness as a key leadership characteristic is generally recognized. Knowledge is the foundation for good decision making, and data provide the catalyst that makes reliable discernment possible. So, the collection and analysis of data become an important leadership tool. Gathered facts provide information for making choices. Without the knowledge that data bring, the resulting decision becomes nothing more than speculation. Data and the understanding they create facilitate prediction—the ability to plan with assurance that goals can be realized. Leadership is, at its core, all about prediction: defining a course for the future.

Because variability is a fact of life, its influence is continually at work. This chapter looks at a fundamental form of data analysis that is based on the tendency of events, or the measures that can be derived from those events, to distribute themselves in normal patterns. Researchers for years have been using this phenomenon by applying simple statistical techniques to assess the adequacy of outcomes.

Accordingly, the discussion here is centered on the normal distribution and an expansion first laid down by Walter Shewhart in the 1920s and then expanded further by individuals such as W. Edwards Deming, Joseph Juran, and Armand Feigenbaum. Although these men are known for applying these ideas to manufacturing processes, the concepts are valid for analyzing many types of data and are useful in many organizational settings. The humble act of aggregating the differences between point-to-point variables, then calculating an average and plotting the distribution of the data points around the average, can reveal causal events. The reason for devoting a whole chapter to this idea is simple. It is a powerful tool for understanding capriciousness and for detecting events that may be indications of system problems.

For some managers, there is often a tendency to look at just two data points (e.g., this month's sales are down from last month's) and decide that something needs to be done. The uncovered dip in sales, however, may be nothing more than normal variability at work, and blowing the whistle will do nothing other than make people jump. Two-point comparisons do not predict trends and are much like rolling the dice. Having the same or a higher amount appear is chance and contingent on many other forces that act on the sales process. Getting people to jump once too often can diminish enthusiasm and the future inclination to problem solve, particularly when nothing new is discoverable.

Industry, and particularly manufacturing, in recent years has begun to recognize the value of measurement and analysis as a means for maintaining process stability. On the other hand, nonmanufacturers have tended to collect only financial measurements, using the rationale that the outputs from administrative and staff functions cannot be easily evaluated. Managers in many cases seem to believe that services, unlike products, do not have distinct practices or well-defined features that can be readily characterized for measurement. Without system-wide measurements, however, effective planning and decision making become tentative activities based mostly on sentiment and perception. In such cases, the chance of satisfying customers and maintaining the soundness of work processes is mostly a hit-or-miss venture. Some ideas will work, but many others will require an excuse or apology.

A major consideration when collecting data is the selection and use of measurements. As a start, the purpose or reason for doing something—its goals and future expectations—must be clearly defined. The indicators chosen should have a system perspective and best represent those characteristics that will lead to customer satisfaction, improved resource utilization, operational efficiencies, or employee well-being. An organization's performance measurements should focus on inputs, key process events, and resulting outputs. These indicators should create a balanced score card for aligning activities and ensuring value for customers and stakeholders. When using a balanced scorecard, both financial and nonfinancial measurements assume equal importance and are part of the assessment system at all organizational levels. When Kaplan and Norton (1996) introduced the concept of a balanced scorecard, their notion was to measure organizational performance from more than a financial viewpoint. The idea was to link long-term strategies with short-term goals. Subsequently, the idea has been applied in many settings to give a better picture of overall business operations.

When developing performance measurements, look for indicators that assess proximity to standards, uniformity and stability of processes, customer satisfaction, and employee effectiveness. Assess multiple business functions and link key measurements to strategic objectives. There should be a mix of outcome and process characteristics. Do not focus exclusively on financial dimensions, but instead focus on those factors that will create long-term value. Examine the cause-and-effect relationships that follow activities through a system or process, beginning with customer requirements, followed by process inputs, process activities, process realization, delivery, and finally customer service. Choose measurements that lead to remedial and preventive actions rather than fixing up and correcting after the fact.

Data are a collection of measurements on which conclusions can be drawn and decisions made. The following are some basics to consider when working with data:

- Processes produce data that are measurable and recordable.
- Data are variable; they differ from hour to hour and day to day.
- Data variability produces patterns that can be used to assess process predictability.
- Data collection and analysis aid problem solving.
- Data do not become information until they are collected and analyzed.
- Data gathering and analysis permit you to speak in terms of fact.

To be of value, data must be relevant, reliable, and representative. Selected measurements should be based on what is important to you and your customers and produce results that are repeatable and predictable, so that when exceptions occur, meaningful improvement becomes possible. Data can come from observations or opinions but should be measured at various points over time and at various process locations to ensure validity. Opinion data are typically survey data; observable data come from attributes that can be measured, counted, or categorized.

Successful and meaningful data collection starts with a purpose and answers why, what, where, when, who, and how. This inquiry needs to start before beginning data collection. The following are some questions that should be answered to better ensure the data collected are relevant, reliable, and representative:

- Why are the data being collected?
- What data will be collected?
- What data collection tools and methods will be used?
- Where should data collection take place?
- When will data be collected and for how long?
- Who will be responsible for collecting data?
- Who will compile and analyze data collection results?
- How will the data be collected?
- How will we know the right data have been collected?

Collecting the wrong data will produce meaningless results. Being data driven is not enough. Data collection must have purpose, examine critical attributes, and provide for analysis that has relevance. Do not collect data for the sake of having data. Instead, collect meaningful data. Collecting, organizing, and then analyzing data is time consuming. Do not burn out process owners and customers by collecting data that do not describe essential process characteristics. Before beginning data collection, make sure the reasons are clear and take time to plan for data collection and analysis. Collect only what is important for understanding the process or solving a problem, avoiding the tendency to measure too many variables or attributes that are irrelevant. Anywhere between two and four indicators in any given category being measured should be sufficient. So, think about critical measurements—finding those key indicators that will act as a thermometer for organizational wellness (Schultz, 2006).

The benefit of measurement and analysis is the ability to contextualize issues—develop a picture through calculation or charts and graphs—so decisions and predictions have a certain level of confidence. Unfortunately, however, many people believe data analysis and the statistics produced are not relevant as a competency for leadership. They can point to examples in which individuals have made it to the top with only a cursory regard for numerical information. The ability to understand more than the dollar value of process contingencies, however, sets people with four-cornered competencies—profound knowledge—apart from the crowd. These individuals have a tool that allows them to truly see trends and then act when action is really needed.

System Ups and Downs Are a Matter of Routine

All systems and processes are impacted and influenced by variability. That is all right because life and work have their inherent inconsistencies—ups and downs. Although much of human endeavor is about creating consistency, there is a continual cascade of inputs that push and pull events so outputs differ one from another. Sometimes, the drift is excessive and noticeable; at other times, the change is modest and imperceptible. Variability is a fact of life, and its impacts have shaped the world and its nature, creatures, and environment. Most of the time, these inconsistencies are tolerable and a matter of routine; we have learned to live with them. However, on other occasions, these forces are intolerable and produce only troubling results that can have chaotic consequences.

Take, for example, the tasks that comprise the daily ritual of preparing for and getting to work. Each component has its time-consuming activities, which for the most part are routine and automatic. Little thought is given to how much time is spent on each pursuit, and the cumulative effect is rarely considered until some intervening event or special cause interrupts the habitual chain of events. If timed and recorded, however, these individual and sequential activities vary from day to day by several seconds and often minutes. Taken as a whole, these differences have little meaning because they have become tolerable and are matter of fact—just a consequence of getting to work. Yet, periodically, by chance, one of these trivial activities turns into a time-consuming event that lays the whole routine to waste. In these cases, we recognize the problem and take action or accommodate it because events are beyond our control.

There are two sources for variation acting on this work-prepping process and all processes. The first source includes influences that are predictable and typically stable. We anticipate and live with them. These are called "common-cause variations" and can be described as follows:

■ The effect is always present in the process, although the influence varies from time to time.
■ The individual impact is usually small.
■ Cumulative impacts can be large but are typically predictable.

Then, there are those influences that are sporadic and unpredictable. They create conspicuous disorder in the daily scheme of things. These are called "special-cause variations" and can be described this way:

■ The effect is not always present in the process, and the influence is infrequent.
■ The cause comes from outside the familiar process, and the impact can be either small or large.
■ The stimulus combines with normal variation to create an impact that is large and distorts individual common causes.

What does this mean, and why is it important? There is a tendency to misinterpret variation and react to its causes inappropriately. These mistakes come in two forms, which can be costly because reactions, although intuitive, are often counterproductive and do not improve process or system outcomes. Instead, these events intensify the situation. The first mistake happens when reaction to a routine source of variation is treated as a special cause, an outside occurrence, but in reality the influence was the result of normal activity or common-cause variation. The second mistake happens when reaction to an outside source of variation is treated as a common cause, a routine occurrence, but the actual influence was the result of nonroutine activity or special-cause variation.

Businesses, for instance, collect a wealth of information about sales, expenses, and shipments. Well-meaning managers, however, often evaluate these numbers using a point-to-point comparison between a budgeted standard or a previous set of figures and the current set of data. If the result is positive, then all is assumed to be well. If the result is negative, then there is a call for action. Unfortunately, the assumptions are often wrong and irrational because the basis for comparison did not reflect the system's true nature, including ever-present and inherent variability: the tendency for results to move up as well as down in a normal pattern.

Rewarding or praising positive results that are an expression of normal variability creates disincentives. It encourages confidence and a continued course of action when an alternative or more robust effort might be required to sustain or improve process realities. Likewise, criticizing or punishing the negative effects of common-cause variation produces an undercurrent of resentment because people recognize the futility of problem solving when there is nothing to uncover. A sense of apathy sets in when a call to arms finds only routine ambiguities. Then, when real trouble is discovered, the workforce is slow to react, and abatement can become a protracted process.

Treating special causes as if they are normal can also have consequences. Here is an example:

> Over the last two months, a second-tier supplier to the recreational vehicle industry experienced an unusual increase in orders. The sales department believes the customer responsible for the boost is anticipating difficulty in labor negotiations and is overstocking in case there is a strike. This customer has been slowly increasing orders along with planning to bring in outside labor if there is a work stoppage. Meanwhile, due to the demand, manufacturing at the supplier facility has been increased by adding temporary labor and expanding hours. However, it now appears orders are beginning to wane, but at the insistence of the sales department, production is continuing at an unabated clip although the warehouse is filling up.

Here is another recognizable case in point:

> A community bank had for several years been able to sell mortgage loan contracts in the secondary market without concern for down payment and income requirements typically used when screening potential borrowers. The secondary market representative kept calling and asking for any new mortgage loans the bank could send its way. The bank president saw this as a growth possibility and indicated to the loan department that the customary requirements for obtaining mortgages could be stretched. He insisted this was a low-risk opportunity, and that any inherent liabilities were being buffered through mechanisms for collateralizing loans in the secondary marketplace. But, when the housing bubble deflated, it became clear that many loans were in jeopardy because buyers of questionable quality were not able to make their payments.

Special-cause variation can be misread because it appears as an opportunity and is then optimistically accepted as normal. The likelihood of consequential results are ignored and not acted on until system distortions become really troublesome. Upward movement does not necessarily mean everything is satisfactory, particularly when the resulting numbers or indicators signaling what is considered normal and usual reality are being breached. For instance, individuals who invested with Bernard Madoff at some point recognized their situation was not typical, but failed to ask why because they thought that ever and always upward was good. Too much of a good thing, however, means probability is being challenged, there is a risk of undetected problems, and at some point downward pressure will prevail. Abnormality, whether positive or negative, is a signal that it is time to study essential system characteristics for causes and answer the question: Why is this happening?

Yes, system ups and downs are a matter of routine because an assortment of inputs and pressures continually act on underlying processes. Not recognizing the influence of variability, or misreading its sources and then acting inappropriately, however, typically leads to calamity. The results are increased costs, reduced performance, lower quality, and ultimately loss of customer or stakeholder confidence. As a remedy, the leader needs to understand variability, its attributes and consequences, and then learn when to act so the system can remain stable over the long term. Relying on intuition or perception is not the solution, but acting on the signs embedded in system highs and lows is an approach that is more insightful and less speculative. Variability is a fact of life. Learn its messages and how to apply its lessons.

Visualizing Process Variability

A change in value from one reporting period to another, although an indicator of process variability, does not necessarily mean movement upward is better or movement downward is worse. Two-point comparisons show only that something is more or less than the previous condition but provide no history, no context to assess normality and thus indicate

Table 5.1 Sales Data

January to June Sales (in thousands of dollars)							
Product Line	January	February	March	April	May	June	Total
Product A	500	600	700	600	400	300	3,100
Product B	100	100	150	200	200	350	1,100
Product C	350	250	200	200	150	100	1,250
Product D	250	100	150	80	50	60	690
Total	1,200	1,050	1,200	1,080	800	810	6,140

something unusual is happening or there is a need to do something different. Process characteristics can be viewed and displayed in a number of ways. Typically, this is done by placing numerical values in columns or in tables where discerning a meaning can be visually difficult. Differences can be detected, but understanding magnitude, trends, or what the data mean cannot be done without further manipulation or calculation. Table 5.1 illustrates a typical presentation of sales data.

Although tables organize and present relevant data, the arrangement of information tends to encourage limited compressions: June sales are down from January. While it is easy to contrast one number with another, the meaning or context is not readily visible. Is the difference significant? Does it represent a trend, or are the monthly variations reasonable and within normal expectations? Unfortunately, without meaningful references, judgment becomes a matter of speculation.

Displaying numerical data in a chart or graph attracts attention and makes the information visually consumable. Relative magnitude and frequency become perceptible, and comparisons are more easily made. A well-presented graph unlocks numerical relationships that are difficult to see in table form, as shown in Figure 5.1. In this case, sales figures for the various product lines can be displayed in several ways. Figure 5.1 is a cumulative bar chart summarizing sales by product line for the year's first 6 months. Figure 5.2, on the other hand, is

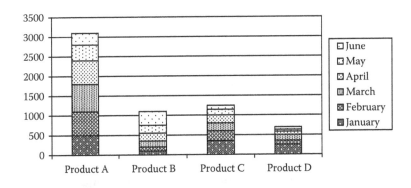

Figure 5.1   Cumulative bar chart, January to June sales (in thousands of dollars).

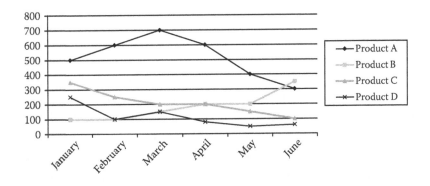

Figure 5.2   Line chart, January to June sales (in thousands of dollars).

a line chart that compares sales for all four product lines in time-ordered sequence. Although the intent of each chart is different, the variability of sales from month to month is readily visible. Whether these ups and downs are significant or meaningful is a matter for further discussion that is addressed in the next section. Data, however, that are displayed in a chart create a visual context that reduces the tendency to make point-to-point comparisons.

The bar chart (cumulative data plot) and line chart (time-ordered plot) tell different stories. The bar chart evaluates different categories of data using a comparable measurement; the time-related chart shows the variability of data as events occur.

Figure 5.3   Run chart example that displays data in sequence.

The time-ordered sequence presents a running record of a process characteristic in a context that can be used to understand process health: whether process conditions are normal or whether circumstances exist for which corrective action is required.

Data that are associated with time (e.g., information associated with many business operations) can be visualized in a simple time-ordered chart that portrays process variability. This running record is usually called a run chart. Typically, the horizontal axis is associated with time and the vertical axis depicts change in value, such as dollars. Figure 5.3 illustrates a hypothetical run chart that displays data in sequence. Run charts can monitor the performance of one or more processes over time to detect trends, shifts, or cycles.

Charted data in this example are weekly sales in thousands of dollars for an imaginary product. The amounts are recorded in the order in which sales occurred. The progression is in weeks, but depending on the application, it could be hours, days, or months. In most circumstances, this is a fairly simple technique to assess performance measures for trends or patterns. Typically, 20 to 25 data points are needed to make a meaningful interpretation. To obtain sufficient information, a plot of this nature can be started using historical data and can conclude with current data.

Time-plotted data can be measurements, such as capacity, size, or dimension. The information can be counts, such as amounts, number of occurrences, or quantities. If, however, there were many events in a short time span (such as incoming telephone calls or time waiting on hold during a 30-minute period), then computing an average and plotting that average point would be more appropriate. By ordering data in time sequence, the extent of natural or normal variation becomes visible, as do unusual or abnormal events.

In the example in Figure 5.3, several conditions are readily evident. First, normal variability—the highs and lows from week to week—is fairly consistent, running somewhere in the range of $15,000 to $22,000 with data points fairly evenly distributed above and below the average. In addition, there are no trends, as depicted by sequential points running up or down. Second, however, there are 2 weeks with sales above the norm, one well above at $32,000 and one slightly above at $25,000. That is nice to see, but such events should raise the question, Why? If these points were below the average, someone would most likely be called to the sales manager's office. In any case, unusual events should be investigated even when positive. Why did this happen, and can we do it again? Or, was it fluke? Is someone stocking up because a strike is impending? This may mean trouble with sales of Product A at some point down the road.

Another example, Figure 5.4, for a make-believe product presents a slightly different picture and raises some interesting

Figure 5.4   Run chart example with indicators that offer the chance for problem solving.

questions. Again, the data are fairly evenly distributed around the average line. However, the overall variability is rather large—the spread from low to high, $7,000 to $20,000 shows an inconsistent picture. Also, during the last 8 weeks there has been a shift in sales as depicted by at least seven points in a row at or above the average line. These signals raise the following question: Why? Was this a new territory or product that needed time to settle in, or is there something else going on? These indicators provide an opportunity for problem solving— real problem solving.

This is not the time to jump on the sales representative, but an occasion to study what is happening by gathering additional information if data that are gathered and charted do not present an acceptable picture. Average sales for Product B, for example, should be closer to those for Product A. Demanding more and pressuring the salesperson to do better, however, without first understanding underlying causes will not bring about improvement. When people are under pressure to meet a target, and they recognize they have no control over prevailing circumstances, one of two things will happen. Either the data will be distorted or the system or process will be distorted and compromised. The most productive way to use data is through problem solving that truly looks for root causes.

Data in this case may be a harbinger of trouble but do not indicate where the problem lies. Information used as a stick to prod people already doing their best gains nothing. Instead, using data collection results as a means for problem solving, with workers allowed to diagnose issues and resolve them, produces both learning and bona fide improvement.

Measurement, analysis, and improvement work best in an environment in which there is trust and a realization that data are being used to seek improvement, not blame. When data are collected under conditions of fear and distrust, outcomes will, in most cases, not reflect true issues or concerns, and some facts may remain hidden, buried, or unreported. Instead, judgments will tend to reflect a biased notion about conditions or the people working in the system rather than about what is really occurring. Meaningful improvement is not likely to happen, which can have an impact on long-term prospects for efficiency, quality, and customer satisfaction. Data provide a voice for the system and the processes that occur within it. These messages can be used to monitor and improve practices so outcomes indeed match expectations. Here are some simple guidelines for assessing process variation:

■ Avoid considering every successive movement in measurement as significant.

■ Collect 20 to 25 data points and plot them relative to time so an overall picture of variability can be established. Once this baseline is established, subsequent points can be added and compared to existing measurements. Use historical data to create a starting point but add new data to create a running perspective.

■ Calculate an average and indicate it visually to provide a context for routine variation.

■ Investigate points that are discernibly beyond routine variation.

■ Investigate shifts in the process, as suggested by seven points in a row above or below the average.

■ Investigate trends, suggested by six points in a row moving up or down.

■ Investigate whether the spread in process variability looks too good to be true. Someone may be cooking the numbers.

■ Investigate if the spread in variability widens beyond what has been routine or might be acceptable to customers and usual process activities. This may mean someone is tampering with the process and making uninformed adjustments.

These signals indicate exceptions to the usual system or process tendency, announcing to those who work in the process that steps should be taken to identify and correct the causes that created the condition. Initiate problem solving that will change and improve the underlying process dynamics.

Process Behavior Chart

The process behavior chart has many similarities to the run chart but mathematically defines the normal limits for variability and places them on the chart. The reason for doing this is made clear in this section. Often, people have uneasiness when computations are required. They throw up their hands or develop a glassy-eyed stare when an equation is presented. So, if you are intimidated by statistical analysis or feel anything other than calculating percentages is too difficult, then jump ahead to the next section. The concepts, however, are not that tough to understand, and average working people with nothing more than a calculator have learned how to use these techniques effectively to diagnose system and process issues. Why not stay on board just to see whether there is something you might learn from the discussion in this section.

Business data are often associated with time. The time-ordered record becomes a valuable analytical tool and is the best method for displaying facts, then interpreting process behavior. Almost all business measures can be organized in time sequence and when plotted will show a history of variability. The reasons for these fluctuations are many. The process or system creating the data is influenced by numerous cause-and-effect relationships, which in turn produce a running record of differing values. Although the chart readily displays the ups and downs of daily activity, deciding whether a particular high or low is significant requires some further insight and rules for decision making. As a start to developing a context for making sense of variation, the following are concepts to keep in mind:

- All processes are subject to external and internal pressures that create displayable variation.
- Some variation is routine; it demonstrates repeatable and predictable results that are characterized as common-cause events.
- Some variation is exceptional; it demonstrates erratic and inconsistent results that are differentiated as special-cause events.
- Measured results can be charted in a time-ordered plot with computed limits that will allow distinction between common and special causes of variation.

The calculated limits create a horizontal band that provides a sense of history and a context for deciding whether to take action. It is a road of sorts that defines what to expect. This type of chart records process or system behavior over time and frames the plotted ups and downs with limits that can be used for predicting and assessing past as well as future performance. The technique developed by Shewhart is used most often to monitor and control manufacturing processes. These ideas, however, are applicable to any process in which time-ordered measures can be obtained and can minimize the risk of misdiagnosing cause-and-effect relationships. The calculated and displayed limits indicate the edges of normality and help distinguish between common-cause and special-cause variation. The normal limits for variation, often called control limits, provide guidance for action—when to do something or let the process continue. Figure 5.5 is an example of a process behavior chart, typically called a control chart.

In this example, which displays sales dollars (m) in thousands and the lower natural limit (LNL) and upper natural limit (UNL), variability over 30 months is immediately recognizable. The ups and downs are fairly evenly distributed around the average. Some months sales are lower than others, but there was always a recovery. There were no trends or large shifts

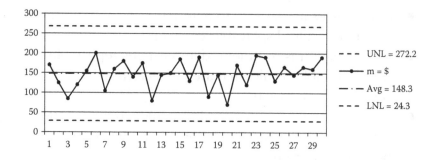

Figure 5.5   Process behavior chart.

indicating something out of the ordinary was happening. Sales have behaved consistently for more than two years. The ebb and flow appear to be a regular consequence of doing business under a particular set of conditions. Although there are limits for normal variation displayed on the chart, changeability falls within a narrow range and has been repeatable and predictable for some time. Questioning the down months and enforcing some sort of action would have gained nothing because natural forces were already in play for more robust sales in a later month.

Creating a chart of this nature does not require a degree in higher mathematics. Skilled workers, with just a bit of training and a handheld calculator, routinely construct and interpret process behavior charts. It is relatively easy and painless, a practice that becomes clear after several trial runs. Table 5.2 and the accompanying calculations illustrate the basics for creating a chart that is capable of tracking process behavior. The concepts are statistically based and set the limits for the dispersion of data around a process average using many point-to-point comparisons. In other words, the data displayed in the table are evaluated one after another by calculating the absolute difference between adjacent values. The positive or negative sign is ignored, and the resulting value is called the range. Here is the range calculation:

$$r = |m_a - m_b|$$

Table 5.2 Calculating Process Behavior

Sample	Measurement (Thousands of Dollars)	Range	Sample	Measurement (Thousands of Dollars)	Range
1	170		16	130	55
2	125	45	17	190	60
3	85	40	18	90	100
4	120	35	19	145	55
5	155	35	20	70	75
6	200	45	21	170	100
7	105	95	22	120	50
8	160	55	23	195	75
9	180	20	24	190	5
10	140	40	25	140	50
11	175	35	26	165	25
12	80	95	27	155	10
13	145	65	28	165	10
14	150	5	29	160	5
15	185	35	30	190	30
Totals	2,175	645	Totals	2,275	705

where *m* is *measurement* which yields an absolute value. The resulting negative or positive sign is disregarded.

For example,

$$Range = \left| 85_{sample3} - 120_{sample4} \right| = 35$$

The following calculations are used to convert the table information into values that can be used in a time-ordered process behavior chart:

$$Average\ measurement = \bar{X} = \frac{\sum m}{n} = \frac{2175 + 2275}{30} = 148.3$$

$$Average\ range = \bar{R} = \frac{\sum r}{n} = \frac{645 + 705}{29} = 46.6$$

$$Upper\ natural\ limit = UNL = \bar{X} + (2.66 \times \bar{R})$$

$$= 148.3 + (2.66 \times 46.6) = 272.0$$

$$Lower\ natural\ limit = LNL = \bar{X} - (2.66 \times \bar{R})$$

$$= 148.3 - (2.66 \times 46.6) = 24.3$$

where

m	= *measurement*
n	= *number of values*
$\bar{X}$	= *average measurement*
$\bar{R}$	= *average range*
UNL	= *upper natural limit*
LNL	= *lower natural limit*
2.66	= *scaling factor*
r	= *range*
Σ	= *to sum.*

The intent here is not to make the reader fluent in the construction of charts, but to drive home the fact that data viewed in contextual chunks over time have meaning. Charting the distribution of measurements provides a basis for decision making that is grounded in statistical thinking, has rules for interpreting variation, and reduces the exposure to failures that are the result of guesswork or gut feeling. For a more in-depth look at data analysis using charts, see Donald Wheeler's book *Making Sense of Data* (2003).

Interpreting Process Behavior

Guidance for action is the reason for charting information using a time-ordered approach. Unusual conditions can be detected and an appropriate call to investigate issued. Decisions based on data-driven inference are more likely to be taken seriously and in turn counter the notion that management is continually reinventing the wheel.

The logic supporting process behavior charts is based on empirical evidence that shows virtually all routine variation will distribute observations (data points) around a process average and within calculated natural limits. These limits are at plus or minus three standard deviations from the average. The standard deviation, often called a sigma, is a convenient and quantifiable method for measuring the dispersion of data. It is based on the average deviation of various data points from the process average. The resulting statistic is then adjusted for sample size using a bias correction factor. The operation for converting data that are capable of constructing a time-ordered behavior chart, an individuals chart (I-chart), is as follows:

$$3 \; Sigma = 3\frac{\bar{R}}{d_2} = \frac{3\bar{R}}{1.128} = 2.66 \times \bar{R}$$

where
  d_2 = the sample size correction factor
  3 *Sigma* indicates three standard deviations
  $\bar{R}$ = *average range.*

Thus, the equations

$$UNL = \bar{X} + \left(2.66 \times \bar{R}\right)$$

$$LNL = \bar{X} - \left(2.66 \times \bar{R}\right)$$

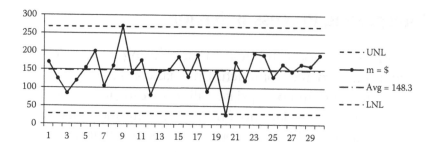

Figure 5.6   Point outside the limits.

It is hoped the preceding discussion makes some sense, but if it does not, consider this: Under normal conditions, data points tend to cluster in bands around the average. Observed experience indicates that in this situation, approximately 70 percent of the values will fall on either side of average or centerline within bands that are one-third of the distance from the average to the calculated natural limits. Conversely, only 30 percent of the values will fall in the areas that are close to the upper and lower limits. This means observed values in a time series plot should be randomly but normally distributed around the average as depicted in Figure 5.6, with 15 percent and 35 percent below the average line, then 35 percent and 15 percent above the average line. If the distribution is not normal and does not produce these percentages, then something is amiss, and an investigation should be started.

Here are some rules for detecting the intrusion of forces that are not routine and normal, signals that indicate special-cause variation is at play in the process:

> *Points outside the limits:* Any single point that is beyond an upper or lower limit is a strong indicator that a special cause is present and will have a dominant impact on process operations. Examples would be if there were an unusual number of shipments in a single day or the percentage of on-time shipments really dropped during a particular week. Whatever the case, these events should

be looked at and a determination made. Does something need fixing, or can the favorable indications be duplicated? Figure 5.6 illustrates this condition.

Run near the limits: Four of five consecutive points on the same side of the average are all within a region that is 50 percent of the distance from either limit. This arrangement indicates a shift in process characteristics and the presence of a moderate but sustained effect from a special cause. Again, ask why this is happening. Why did we have a loss in sales during this period? Figure 5.7 demonstrates this situation.

Trend either up or down: Six consecutive points or more are either increasing or decreasing. This composition indicates the process is being impacted by a moderate but sustained special cause that is creating a slow change in either favorable or unfavorable qualities. Investigate so positive effects can be replicated and negative effects corrected. Figure 5.8 depicts this circumstance.

Run above or below the average: The grouping of seven or more consecutive points on the same side of the average indicates that a weak but sustained special cause is acting on the process, producing either a positive or a negative shift in operations. Both conditions should be studied to assess reasons. Figure 5.9 replicates this effect.

Points clustered near the average: Fourteen consecutive points alternate up and down in close vicinity to the

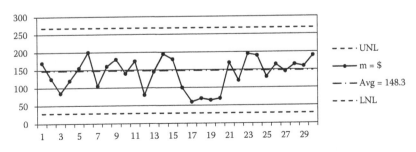

Figure 5.7   Run near the limits.

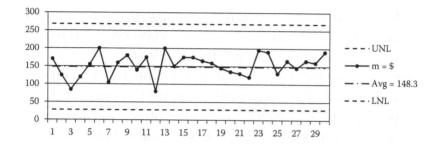

Figure 5.8 Trend either up or down.

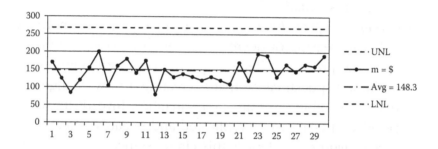

Figure 5.9 Run above or below the average.

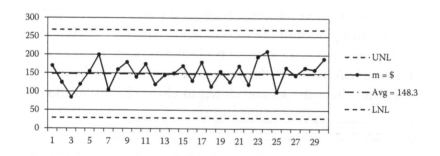

Figure 5.10 Points clustered around the average.

average. This array indicates an advantageous special cause or edited data creating an illusion that everything is fine. Investigate causes so good effects can be reproduced or erroneous information corrected. Figure 5.10 illustrates this condition.

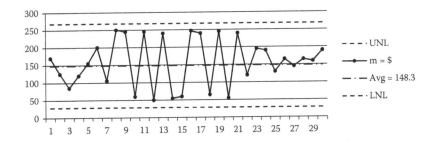

Figure 5.11   Points clustered near the limits.

Points clustered near the limits: Fourteen consecutive points alternating up and down cluster near the process limits. This display indicates that two sources of unreconciled data are being used to document process characteristics or a well-intentioned but misguided individual is tampering with the system or process. Intuitive but unqualified adjustments are being made to one or more process inputs, creating unintended fluctuations. Figure 5.11 demonstrates this effect.

Why is all this ritual and effort necessary? The answer is because there is a tendency to think of performance data in a singular context, to compare this month's average to last month's or to compare this month's sales against last year's sales and thus make an impulsive judgment about operating conditions. Typically, if the difference is positive, then performance is usually considered satisfactory, but if the difference is negative, then performance is frequently judged inadequate.

It would be nice if decision making were so easy. The world is more complex, however—full of inherent and capricious forces. Unfortunately, these details are often ignored when assessing the adequacy of process activities. Managers instinctively react when two consecutive data points show a change by exalting positive occurrences and disparaging negative occurrences, thinking that two points predict a trend. The results, however, are often costly. People are unduly criticized, and programs are initiated that do not produce results. Even more important, however, actual failures and opportunities requiring corrective action are needlessly overlooked.

This point-to-point thinking ignores the numerous pressures that influence system and process stability. Hour after hour and day after day, the components, activities, and resources that produce process and system outcomes are fluctuating. For example, vendors are added and dropped from a list of preferred providers, purchased supplies and components behave or respond with slight differences, old equipment is less accurate and needs more maintenance while new and more efficient equipment is being added, new hires with less training and experience are performing alongside more practiced employees, and environmental conditions of heat, cold, and humidity are affecting equipment and employee performance. These factors and others cause measurable and discernible changes over time.

Living with variation is an everyday occurrence. It is the result of system conditions and relationships that are commonly accepted as part of doing business. At times, however, the changeability can be intolerable and can wreak havoc on system performance. These exceptions are caused by nonroutine process conditions. By measuring and tracking variations in relation to time, the trends and patterns that can assist with decision making become evident. The goal of time series measurement is to differentiate the common and predictable from the unique and unpredictable so meaningful adjustments can be made. If the notion of calculating natural process limits seems cumbersome, then at least plot critical process measures in time-ordered fashion and observe how data points distribute themselves around an average. Look for those inconsistencies that signal variability that is not normal. Basically, the same rules apply when analyzing either run charts or process behavior charts.

There is one more situation that warrants discussion and is frequently encountered when a process is behaving normally (is subject to common-cause variation) but overall output is not acceptable or the spread in variability is simply too much— too wide. In other words, normal process operations are not producing what the business needs or the customer wants. For example, the dollar value of items being shipped, although routine, is not sufficient to sustain current expenses, or the spread in outgoing quality means some customers are receiving marginal products that may be subject to return. The process is repeatable and predictable but not capable of doing what is needed.

Outcomes displayed as figures and patterns are a reflection of what the process in its current state is capable of doing. Opting for better characteristics without improving the process and its basic properties is just wishful thinking. Arbitrarily setting an advantageous target and new process limits, then exhorting the workforce to meet these goals will produce only frustration and failure. Unproductive operations and the resulting data will not change until an informed and studied effort is made to upgrade underlying fundamentals. This means real problem solving and experimentation to determine what type of corrective action will produce the best effects. The competency needed in this case is visionary thinking, not slogan-driven positive thinking. Pragmatic leadership that can guide the often-tedious but difficult tasks of problem resolution and solution implementation should be applied.

Tampering Can Be Costly

Going from a troubled and underperforming situation to one that is settled and productive is not easy. Discovery, planning, and realization take effort, skill, resources, and time. So, there is an overwhelming temptation to instinctively fiddle with inputs and process activities in the hope of finding a timelier and less-consuming way to make changes. This innate meddling is called tampering: making well-meaning but impulsive corrections. All of the following actions are instinctive and intuitive, but they fail to consider how variation can be unintentionally multiplied to create distortions and unintended consequences:

- A manager develops this year's budget based on last year's expenses without considering current goals or projected demand.
- Work standards are continually changed—requiring new levels of output—to reflect increasing demands on the system without changing the means for generating that level of production.
- A worker is continually asked to adjust a process based on the characteristics of the last item produced. The characteristics of that item are the product of conditions at a particular moment in time. The next item produced may be the same but can also be slightly different—larger or smaller—because it is influenced by conditions at a different point in time. Adjustment without knowledge (understanding the distribution of characteristics and why conditions are what they are) will only accentuate the difference in output measurement, thus reducing repeatability and predictability.
- The tax code is continually changed so powerful interest groups can be accommodated. Changes without considering the whole system create distortions and inequities. This is certainly the picture today.
- The last board cut is used as the pattern for the next board to be cut. Because there is the possibility of a slight difference in the previous cut from the actual standard, the mistake can be transferred and become cumulative.
- Managers and employees are rewarded during years when sales and revenue are high; however, this practice fails to recognize that prosperity may not be the result of company acuity, just general economic activity.

The real challenge for a leader is to understand cause-and-effect relationships—having the courage to let the system or process run without tinkering so a true baseline can be recorded. Then, use what has been discovered as the launching pad for problem solving or, as the case may be, recognize that the fluctuations displayed are the result of normal variability so attention can be directed to improvement that reduces variation and increases overall productivity. Both these situations present an opportunity. One corrects and maintains a predictable status quo; the other moves the process toward a new level of capability. The type of action required in each case becomes evident because there is knowledge based on data not guesswork, intuition, or hunches. This use of data, however, requires a basic understanding of the different sources for process and system variability.

The sources for unevenness are based on the inputs and activities that generate process or system outputs. Typically, these influences are categorized as financial resources, material resources, facilities, equipment, methods, people, social and political forces, and environmental factors. All exert pressure and create fluctuations that can be measured, tracked, and studied to assess stability or instability. Judgments can be made about whether variation is the result of common-cause or special-cause influences, and the appropriate remedies can be applied: Stable processes are improved, and unstable processes are fixed. Either type of action, however, requires leadership, profound leadership that has a pragmatic and long-term perspective. It should not be an approach shaped by instinctual conclusions grounded in point-to-point comparisons, thus encouraging overreaction and continual adjustments that further destabilize the system or process.

Tampering is costly because it wastes time and chews up resources that do little to fix or improve process and system realities. It provides a sense of false security that something of value is being done. There is action, but the same problems recur several months later. Meetings are called, the customers are calmed, the returns are fixed. The crisis is subdued, but the complaints start all over again after a brief period. The continual sense of urgency keeps people scrambling, but improvement is elusive because there is no real learning, problem solving, and upgrading. Workers have the drill down perfectly and robotically spring into action when the alarm is sounded, but after the emergency is over, everyone retreats into a humdrum routine waiting for the next fire call.

Here, for example, is a familiar scenario:

> The vice president of sales routinely exhorts manufacturing to complete open orders and push shipments out the door before each business quarter ends. Then, everyone is baffled when complaints and returns rise during the following months. In addition, manufacturing is charged with a negative labor variance for overtime work, has to deal with higher-than-normal rework, and ends up scratching for work during the first month of each new quarter. All this activity, although justified because quarterly shipments appear consistent, has accomplished nothing. Costs routinely are out of control, corrective actions increase, customer complaints amplify, and the workforce views management as confused and disorganized.

So What?

Leadership is all about making the system function in a consistent, predictable manner and doing what needs to be done with the help of those who work in the system. Leadership also means doing what is right and doing that correctly. Deciding what is correct can be intuitive, or it can be considered. In either case, something is done, but is the resulting action right more than 50 percent of the time? Leaders who want to improve these odds have learned to use data and to read the signals that data can produce when charted in relationship to time. The technique is not new and has usually been applied to manufacturing operations in which definable measurements and attributes can be easily obtained. However, all processes produce measurable characteristics that, when analyzed, can be used to assess stability or closeness to a standard. Table 5.3 describes these measurement types.

Table 5.3 Measurement Types and Their Indicators

Type Of Measurement	Indicators
Timeliness: Used to evaluate how closely promised deadlines matched actual completion. Often expressed as a percentage.	• On-time deliveries • Time to respond to calls • Delay time • Wait time • Down time
Cycle time: Used to evaluate the length of time to complete a specific activity or group of tasks. Usually expressed as an average.	• Elapsed time to complete a project • Time to complete a production cycle • Time from order entry to shipping • Elapsed time to complete a specific number of orders
Productivity: Used to assess output, yield, or efficiency. Can be expressed as a ratio of outputs to inputs and as a count that tells how much or how many.	• Items shipped • Returns compared to shipments • Requests met • Audits performed • Value of resources consumed compared to the value of items completed • Number of items reworked • Items processed
Quality: Used to evaluate the closeness to a standard or specification. Included are assessments of customer satisfaction. Can be expressed as a count or percentage.	• Amount of scrap and rework • Error rate • Number of items outside critical limits • Number of customer complaints • Number of blemishes • Defects per number of items shipped

continued

Table 5.3 (continued) Measurement Types and Their Indicators

Type Of Measurement	Indicators
Costs: Used to evaluate the value of services performed for specific transactions. Typically expressed in dollars. Can be ratios, percentages, or sums.	• Project costs • Project costs compared to budgeted costs • Revision or redesign costs • Rework costs • Maintenance costs • Repair or replacement costs
Utilization: Used to evaluate resources expended based on availability or capacity. Usually applied to equipment, people, or facilities. Primarily expressed as a percentage or ratio.	• Labor rate • Machine utilization rate • Capacity rate • Number of machines down for repair compared to the number operating • Length of time equipment was operational compared to time it was idle

Source: From Schultz, J.R. (2011). *Making it all work: A pocket guide to sustain improvement and anchor change.* New York: Routledge.

The goal of measurement is informed decision making that reduces the chance for mistakes and lowers costs. Considered judgment is possible when the decision maker can distinguish between the sources of variation—whether the process is running normally or being impacted by a special cause. Understanding these distinctions is important when making improvements. The approach in each case is different. Special-cause variation requires problem resolution and corrective action. Common-cause variation, on the other hand, involves breakthrough thinking that will move a process to new levels of proficiency. Both types of variation involve study, experimentation, and the implementation of a solution. Resolving a special-cause influence, however, merely fixes a problem; addressing common-cause consequences can create progress. In either case, the likelihood of success is greatly increased because outcomes are driven by knowledge and not guesswork. The right issues are addressed, and corrective actions really do fix the problem.

Although a process is operating under the influence of common-cause variation—it is repeatable and predictable—this does not mean it should not or cannot be changed. When all is going well, the goal should be improvement—making business functions better so customers and stakeholders are well served. The objective in this case becomes continual advancement, breaking new ground by reducing common-cause variation and by purposely working to tilt the trend line in a positive direction. This will require more than simply setting ambitious targets. A substantial and focused effort is required that changes underlying forces that drive process and system outputs. This means looking at and upgrading those factors that influence customer service (responsiveness, reliability, assurance, empathy, and tangibles) or changing those factors that improve product quality (materials, methods, machinery, people, and workplace surroundings). In short, investigate and improve those issues that make current operations difficult, less productive, less effective, or less efficient. Answer the question, How can we do this better?

The final story in this chapter is about the brewing industry and how understanding and managing process variability made beer drinking enjoyable glass after glass.

> In 1899, Arthur Guinness and Sons hired a statistician name William Gosset. The brewery, and most of the brewing industry at the time, was having trouble ensuring the quality of its product—batch after batch and season after season. Gosset quickly recognized that process stability and the adherence to recipe standards were the answer. So, he embarked on a program that would measure process inputs and activities using small random samples. In addition, Gosset experimented to see how far a sample mean or average could deviate from the accepted process standard before the flavor was considered unacceptable.

His studies and experiments concluded that, indeed, small samples could be used to represent the larger contribution of batch ingredients, and that there were acceptable and unacceptable limits to variability. Gosset developed a statistic, the *t* test, which would measure the calculated distance between the sample mean and the process standard to determine whether inputs were within the range of normal variability or represented an outlier that would spoil the brewing process. Using this knowledge, he also developed strains of barley, yeast, and hops that produced uniform grain, spore, and cone size, as well as consistent flavor, over a wide range of growing conditions.

Gosset's studies were published in the *Biometrika Journal* in 1908 under the name "Student" so other brewers would not recognize Guinness's use of statistics to ensure product quality. Gosset figured out how to separate special-cause variability from common-cause variability and can be considered the father of modern process control. He used this knowledge to reduce costs, increase productivity, and enhance product quality, which were a major contribution in a highly competitive industry.

All processes display variability. Although outputs may appear identical, if quantified and measured, differences will be detected. These differences when plotted in relationship to time will produce a discernible pattern. The configurations tell a story and are a powerful tool for assessing the stability of the process being studied and measured. The patterns can be the result of observations related to sales, shipments, product defects, customer complaints, inventory turnover, accounts receivable turnover, or any variable that can be tracked regularly. The reason is to understand the spread in variability and process stability or instability. The basic statistical techniques that are associated with sampling distributions can be applied to judge conditions. The goal, of course, is to uncover problems and reduce costs. When special-cause variation is removed—by correcting its underlying sources—the process is stabilized, inconsistency is reduced, and corresponding costs are reduced.

Understanding the variability of work is all about knowing when to act and when not to act. As Gosset recognized, this grasp of events starts with knowing what is normal and how far process measures can drift from a central or average measure before customers and stakeholders will be disappointed by the organization's products or services. Stable processes are easier to manage because their outputs are repeatable and predictable. The goal of leadership is stability or recognizing when there is the potential for trouble and initiating action to manage the inconsistencies. The ability to understand and read the ups and downs of variability, quite simply, makes the job of leadership easier.

Chapter 6

Give Meaning, Purpose, and Direction to the Job at Hand

Introduction

All organizations have a purpose and were created because someone or some group thought a particular end was important. Although the desired reason may not be apparent to everyone, members of an organization do work at jobs that have relevant and intended outcomes. The effort, however, may not be well coordinated; therefore, activities may be directed at differing and competing goals. Leaders who can vividly translate the organization's purpose into a unifying and personal vision have a much better chance of getting the workforce focused and moving in a common direction.

This chapter examines why purpose is important and explains how to create a statement of purpose and then how to anchor the purpose as part of the organization's culture. These are the topics that are covered:

- ■ Purpose and why it is important
- ■ Creating the purpose
- ■ Communicating the purpose
- ■ Anchoring the purpose through constancy of action
- ■ Interpreting the organization's purpose through planning
- ■ Appreciating that the job at hand has just begun

Purpose and Why It Is Important

Workplaces are complex, multilevel, and filled with competing demands. Yet, as a functioning enterprise, there is usually one overriding reason for all the striving and hustle that goes on within its walls. Unfortunately, unless the purpose has been fleshed out and specifically stated, individual effort can lose focus and be at odds with the efforts of other equally motivated well-meaning people. When clarity is absent, individuals may act out of confusion and at cross-purposes because each person may have differing ideas about goals and how to achieve them. The organization, although an industrious and thriving center of activity, may not be as competitive, effective, or efficient as its contemporaries.

A common purpose is the catalyst, the compelling tug that can align disparate groups in a shared cause. Having a well-defined purpose lets the workforce know (1) what business the organization is in, (2) where it is headed in the long run, and (3) how to set priorities over the short run so long-term objectives can be met. Knowing and understanding the organization's purpose can mean the difference between just working and working with intention.

The organization must accommodate and appeal to a multitude of communities. The purpose and accompanying mission, vision, and value statements must focus action toward customer needs as well as inform diverse constituent groups that the organization is acting in their best interests. The major groups and their typical needs are described as follows:

- *Customers:* This group receives the output of organizational endeavor. Customers expect goods and services that meet a set of perceived needs for quality, reliability, tangible attributes, responsiveness, empathy, and assurance.
- *Employees:* This group produces the goods and services that an organization provides. Employees expect safe and comfortable work conditions; in addition, they want to be adequately compensated for their efforts. They will also need training and professional development so work can be accomplished effectively and efficiently.
- *Shareholders:* This group has risked capital to help fund organizational expansion and growth. Shareholders expect a return on their outlay that equals or exceeds the prevailing rates that can be received from less-speculative investments. Large investors will often try to influence organizational decisions to ensure an ongoing flow of income.
- *Stakeholders:* This group is impacted by organizational decisions. Stakeholders include suppliers, contractors, and the community at large. These individuals expect to be treated honestly, equitably, and as respected neighbors and community citizens.

All these integral groups have a fundamental need to understand how the organization's future direction will affect their lives. Statements of purpose must therefore clarify the drivers of operational effectiveness, what sacrifices will have to be made, and what the ultimate payoff will be. In short, a well-stated purpose helps others define their relationship with the organization.

In addition, there is a natural tendency for people to be complacent and remain steadfast in the way they conduct their daily activities, particularly when current operations are reasonably effective and nonthreatening. Work groups and their supervisors would rather not rock the boat. These groups have adapted to the current system. Its practices and relationships have become automatic and comfortable. The familiar routines have allowed many employees to create a mental image of their worth that is reassuring and secure. This sense of steadiness produces a feeling of self-satisfaction and a reluctance to do work differently. In this case, a compelling statement about future direction can provide the inspiration for a new mental model and consequently a renewed focus and deliberate effort toward the organization's goals.

Organizational performance can become lackluster because work groups are doing only what needs to be done. Muddled conditions can create a malaise in which enduring the day-to-day vagaries of one's job becomes the focus. There is dissatisfaction with current operations, how processes are managed, and where the organization appears to be headed. People recognize that current direction and effort are being hampered by unsolved problems that remain largely beyond worker control. This invites a survival mentality, with bickering and one-upmanship the norm. Work groups, protecting territory, maximize their effectiveness to the disadvantage of others. Organizations suffering from such disquiet usually manage to stay in business but then tread water as groups struggle for meaning and a unifying sense of direction. Here, a leader with a compelling notion of purpose could challenge immobility by clearly stating where the organization is headed and why the work being done is important.

Creating the Purpose

The ability to set a clear and distinct direction is recognized and cited by some researchers as a defining attribute of leadership. Creating a compelling purpose and a clear vision lets everyone know where the organization is headed and points people in a collective direction. History indicates this capacity to rally others toward a shared objective is an essential characteristic of successful leaders. However, being a visionary does not mean the awareness for a convincing future was devised

in isolation and then rolled out with fanfare and the cry
"follow me." The leadership behavior that people will remember and rally to is inclusion—the feeling that they were part
of the vision-shaping process. Leadership in this context is
really about reading the situation, the environment, the needs
of constituents, and then interpreting and explaining what
should be done. It is about showing a plausible and convincing view of the future and how organizational goals align with
follower expectations.

So, creating a purpose and future sense of direction starts
with understanding the organization—its past, its current status, and where people would like it to be. In essence, the job
of crafting a reason for existence and a future vision that people can rally around is similar to performing a gap analysis.
It starts with raising questions and then having work groups
evaluate and respond with considered answers about nagging
concerns and potential expectations. The process concludes
by distilling the information into a meaningful statement that
will help everyone involved personalize future prospects
for themselves.

The statement of direction or purpose should be more than
a well-structured sentence demanding commitment. It should
convey a worthwhile reason for moving in a new direction
that allows others to have a stake in the future. In addition,
the statement should be specific to current conditions: the
needs of customers, clients, and stakeholders. Neither generic
terms nor statements that are excessive flights of imagination
will work. If that is the case, almost everyone involved will
promptly recognize the announcement for what it is—that the
picture being portrayed is not related to their expectations for
a clear future—and will tune out. A well-designed statement
of purpose should have the following characteristics:

- It is brief so that it can be easily communicated,
  explained, and understood.
- It conveys a picture of the future and the desired end.

- It is clear and focused so decisions produce common results.
- It says something enabling and appealing to customers and stakeholders.
- It is realistic in its intention so the end appears obtainable.

Purpose defined by mission, vision, and value statements—often used in combination—contains related concepts that serve separate objectives. The vision is a banner headline, crisp and to the point, that can be placed on letterheads, on business cards, and in advertisements that immediately identify an ideal image and what the organization intends to do. For example, here are a few vision statements:

- Taking care of business.
- Invent.
- Quality is job one.
- A leader in learning.
- Shared governance in nursing.
- Our job is customer service.

All are a capstone phrase for a deeper underlying philosophy that makes the organization valuable in the eyes of its customers, employees, shareholders, and stakeholders.

On the other hand, the mission statement is a more robust explanation of organizational intent and may contain several sentences, including a description of responsibility and values. Again, however, these statements should be brief and to the point. Do not let the true message be buried in a maze of flowery and often-competing statements that can leave people guessing what it is the organization is trying to accomplish. Here are a few examples of a clearly stated purpose:

- Our college provides accessible high-quality learning experiences that serve the community. We value excellence, respect, and integrity.
- We strive to be a market leader and valued supplier in custom-engineered protective packaging and

material-handling products. We will serve our customers, employees, and shareholders.

■ We will advance the health status of the individuals and communities we serve through high-quality patient care, teaching the next generation of health professionals, and advancing scientific discovery and technology.

The Process and How to Make It Happen

To make the process happen, start with the intention that this endeavor should involve everyone and be informative, open, nonthreatening, and most of all pleasurable. As the leader, take the initiative for creating a shared vision. The workforce may have clues to a common understanding, but because of normal structural barriers and the daily pressure of work, members will not act on their own. Initiate the conversation by asking people to tap into their deeper sense of community, to question, to listen for answers, to reflect on what was learned, and to articulate a shared commitment.

The power of this process and the quality of results will depend on your attitude and the capacity of senior managers to genuinely participate. Being honest and true to intentions is important because saying one thing and then doing otherwise can ultimately undermine this endeavor. It may take several years, but once followers feel betrayed or manipulated toward a contrived end, they will rebel. Work groups will make your life miserable at best and particularly difficult at the extreme. Yes, you are the leader, but only because stakeholder groups feel you can do what needs to be done in everyone's best interest.

Begin by holding a round of organizational meetings at which people can express themselves and honest information can be gathered. Use trusted employees, those who the workforce looks to for guidance and inspiration, as facilitators for the event. Do not depend exclusively on the usual group of executives and assistants, who may be viewed as stewards for the status quo. Look to others who have standing in their own domain regardless of formal position in the hierarchy. Scout for true organizational loyalists who can tap into the enterprise's deeper sense of history. Honest impressions, from people who care greatly about the organization's culture, are the desired result, not someone's filtered feel-good interpretation.

Listen

Hold listening sessions for everyone in the organization. The group size for each session should be somewhere between 20 and 25. Break the groups into teams of five. Ask the following questions and allow time between each question for people to respond:

- What are past attributes that have made this organization what it is? Customer service, quality, a good place to work, or maybe fiscal responsibility are examples.
  - Use the Affinity Technique, a brainstorming technique, to generate, list, and group ideas silently according common themes. A description of this approach appears in the Appendix.
- What are the barriers, the day-to-day practices, that obscure organizational direction? What are intervening activities that can balance and restrain these negative forces?
  - Use the Force Field Analysis technique to identify negative and positive ideas that may work for or against moving in a particular direction. An explanation of this method also appears in the Appendix.
- What legacy would you like to see the organization leave that will help carry it into the future? Again, use the Affinity Technique to gather and group ideas.

Synthesize

The previous sessions will generate several prioritized lists containing ideas and insight about the workforce's closely held feelings. Described will be the good, the bad, and the ugly and where work groups feel the organization ought to be headed. Create a synthesized (shared) statement of purpose that combines the positions and thinking gathered during the listening sessions. The following describes how to sort many ideas into a meaningful few:

- Give copies of the prioritized lists to senior managers and allow several days so the responses can be studied and receive reflection.
- At a joint meeting, ask each executive to summarize his or her feelings, both negative and positive, about the information gathered from the listening sessions. In round-table fashion, record the answers on a flip chart or whiteboard.
- Ask the group to find a common theme, a collective statement of purpose that reflects key ideas derived from the listening sessions. Use the Affinity Technique to consolidate ideas.
- Ask each executive to write a purpose statement and mission and vision statements, then have these read aloud so everyone at the meeting can have a sense for the prevailing frame of mind. You should retain copies for your consideration.

Create

Take several days to review the responses and develop your declaration of purpose: mission and vision statements. Deciding what should be done first will be up to you. Some individuals are good at zeroing in on a key phrase (the vision); others need to construct the larger purpose first (the mission). In the end, you will need to find the vital thread that pulls these statements together. Enlist the help of someone who is good with words, at crafting clear and logical statements—an administrative assistant, fellow executive, or consultant. However, the fundamental concepts should be the result of your learning and ultimate thinking. After all, you are the person who will need to make this work—to rally everyone in the new quest. To create a declaration of purpose, do the following:

■ Present your versions of purpose statements to senior executives for discussion. Encourage critical comments and suggestions but do not expect outright approval.

■ Make modifications if needed. Refinements are just part of the process, but remember you are the one who will have to live with the results and use these statements to unite divergent constituent groups.

■ Once the executive group is satisfied with the declarations of purpose and direction, present this version to the workforce for consideration and comment. Circulate the statements throughout the organization and ask for further input and feedback.

■ As needed, make refinements, but stay true to your core conviction and the organization's deeply held beliefs. Finally, roll out the polished statements of purpose, guiding principles, and future direction.

However, do not expect everyone to embrace these declarations unconditionally. The acceptance and feedback should be normally distributed. Roughly 15 percent of the workforce will enthusiastically start pushing in the new direction—initiating projects and encouraging others to become involved. The majority, around 70 percent, will respond with optimism but also will need to see meaningful developments and some actual results. In addition, this group will require encouragement and help finding opportunities for involvement and will expect guidance in their efforts toward prevailing goals and objectives. Their involvement, conversion, and loyalty will require orchestration and facilitation. Another 10 percent will respond with skepticism and want reassurance the organization is headed in the right direction. These individuals will play a waiting game and delay approval while watching to see what happens. Last, there will be a small group, possibly 5 percent, who will never view this purpose as the right direction. They are by nature contrary and cautious and will need to be persuaded and converted or asked to find a more suitable situation elsewhere. See the discussions by Hunt (1992, p. 48) and Scholtes (1998, p. 223) for further information about the distribution of adapters and resisters.

In any case, do not manipulate the information-gathering and statement development process toward an end that excludes competing and diverse voices. This act of trying to reduce discomfort or lessen feelings of inadequacy or loss of face will only create organizational divisions that can set the stage for subterfuge and forceful pushback. All voices need to be heard even when difficult and vocal. At some point, the outliers and diehards will have to be dealt with, but this is not the time.

Nevertheless, as the person in the forefront on this project, expect to hear a range of stories. Some will be optimistic, but others will not be so pleasant. The negatives have lessons and seeds that, when cultivated, can make the organization a better place to work. The goal is inclusion and creating a universal and shared vision that will guide people to places that may appear difficult. The leader in this case needs to be forthcoming, does not leave individuals guessing, shows stragglers how they fit in, and helps everyone focus on the importance of the goal. Even when people recognize the need for moving in a new direction and the value of getting there, many may not know how to make it happen. The leader defines possibilities, enables supporting processes, and directs people toward the place most would prefer to be.

Communicating the Purpose

Although a substantial effort went into the process of developing and refining the organization's purpose and direction, a majority of individuals will not act on their own initiative.

Getting people to move will take clear communication and purposeful steps. The job of motivation does not stop once a common purpose and shared vision are announced. These ideas must be realized through action: planning and budgeting, organizing and staffing, as well as controlling and problem solving. People will require continued inspiration, facilitation, and organizational structures that enable action toward the desired future.

The task will take both selling and telling. Selling creates the sense of urgency; telling explains the reason why. The campaign should be an ongoing process. It should explain the need, amplify the benefits of moving in a new direction, and rationalize the ease of future operations and the rewards derived by way of change. The goal, of course, is to make the need for change obvious so the people are ready and willing to take a chance on the proposed future. The following are considerations for getting the word out:

- *Use different methods:* An announcement in the company newsletter will not be enough. Often, day-to-day concerns can overshadow a single declaration about purpose and vision. When the message is coming from several different directions, it is not as likely to be ignored. Devices for spreading the word typically include meetings, memos, e-mails, posters, newsletters, and personal contact.
- *Repeat the message at regular intervals:* People will need to be reminded that this initiative is as important as other daily tasks and other work obligations. A continuous dialogue keeps the goal in the forefront and ahead of the clutter from competing messages. The ongoing communication lets people know this change in direction is real and will not go away or be replaced in due time.
- *Focus on the benefits:* Frame the message in reference to customers and stakeholders rather than as the need to

reduce costs or increase profits. People can readily empathize with customers and understand that happy customers are repeat customers, that a drop in customer base can mean a loss in jobs. Describe the ease of operations that will result from making changes. Explain how the proposed transformation will make life better for those working in the new environment.

- *Avoid overselling; instead create buy-in:* Individuals will get on board because the need for progress is ultimately seen as a real benefit and not as a cover for the same old approach. Those asked to make changes will be ready to take a leap of faith if rewards from moving in the new direction appear to outweigh consequences. However, creating an overly optimistic picture or one that is outside recognized realities will not work. People seldom change because of being pushed, told, or warned. Exhortations can make them feel manipulated, and the work group will tune out.

Communicating the purpose and direction also means setting the example. A well-conceived and coordinated program can begin to fall apart when those in charge display behaviors that contradict the proposed new direction. The leader and fellow executives may talk one way but exhibit defensive routines that can choke progression toward the recently promoted objective and do so in the name of positive thinking or because "everyone else" wants it that way. A well-meaning but conflicted management group will champion the purpose, describe its benefits, listen intently, and yet conduct themselves in ways that seem to oppose the spirit of the espoused mission, vision, and values.

Here is an example, adapted from the work of Schultz (2011), that illustrates how good intentions were trumped by defensive behaviors that ultimately destroyed the executive's own position.

Gertrud Grossmund, president of a historically acclaimed college, looking ahead several years to the reaccreditation process, decided to use the recently approved AQIP (Academic Quality Improvement Program) option. The goal of this process was to instill the principles and benefits of continuous quality improvement into the culture of participating colleges and universities.

The program required an organizational self-assessment, the selection of several projects that would improve some of the more pressing issues uncovered during the assessment, and a written portfolio report that identified institutional strengths and weaknesses, the rationale for project selection, lessons learned from project work, and future progress toward continuous improvement. The objectives and method are similar to those used by the Baldrige National Quality Program to determine an organization's ability to deliver world-class performance.

A steering committee was appointed to oversee the project and ensure an open and inclusive process. However, after several months of fruitless discussion on how to proceed and organize the initiative, steering committee participation began to wane. Members ultimately recognized they were nothing more than a figurative assembly asked to rubber-stamp an effort driven—not very nimbly—by the president and some of her staff. The leadership in this case continually questioned committee motives, bored people to distraction with data that were selectively gathered, and chided members for not being positive enough or for wanting to present the college in a less-than-favorable light.

Eventually, those who remained on the steering committee did make an attempt to exercise their responsibility and tried to advance the program by making some decisions and suggesting a plan. However, fearing loss of control, Grossmund dissolved the committee by publicly thanking members for their valuable service. Still not truly understanding the program's purpose and not wanting to admit defeat, she appointed a new "Implementation Committee." These were loyalists accustomed to nodding approval, laughing appropriately, and being disempowered—continually deferring to Grossmund's compelling need to be in control.

As individuals who had been rewarded in the past for staying out of the way, they were incapable of inspiring others. As a result, the Implementation Committee thrashed around while one project after another met with uninspiring results. Project teams struggled under the lack of direction and the pressure to achieve positive results—results that would reflect affirmatively on the college and its staff. The portfolio submitted was purged of negative data and meaningful analysis and portrayed results that were self-serving and less than convincing.

The program destined for failure was ultimately salvaged. In the end, accreditation was achieved but with several outstanding issues that needed further attention. Yet, on receiving the feedback report from the Higher Learning Commission, one of the loyalist vice presidents responded in defiance with this remark: "These people are insulting the hard work and positive things we are trying to achieve around here."

This example shows how people advocating for change can frequently shoot themselves in the foot and undermine their own effort. Discouraging meaningful input in the name of positive thinking stops real learning. By displaying privileged or guarded behavior, a mixed message is sent that cannot be easily explained away. Actions that try to avoid exposure to possible discomfort or obscure lack of know-how can heighten resistance and discourage further risk taking. People in the workforce readily recognize their own vulnerability in these situations and look for defensive strategies that can stop further cooperation. Do not be caught saying one thing and then doing another (Schultz, 2011). Managing results in the name of positive thinking—when the true objective is avoiding personal risk, feelings of inadequacy, and perceived embarrassment—will not produce desired results. Such action will undermine leadership credibility and jeopardize the campaign for a new direction and purpose.

Anchoring the Purpose through Constancy of Action

W. Edwards Deming (1986), in his book *Out of the Crisis,* suggested that constancy of purpose was to stay in business, to provide jobs for people by planning now for products and services that will have a market in the future. The development and communication of a compelling purpose, along with corresponding mission, vision, and value statements, set the organization on a shared path toward predictable short- and long-term goals. However, obtaining these desired results will require a steadiness and a constancy of action.

This means that the leader or managers tasked with planning, organizing, initiating, and controlling actions toward the proclaimed purpose will need to behave in accordance with organizational norms and beliefs. Combined leadership actions must be consistent with the organization's culture. Culture is a set of perceptions—commonly understood but unrecorded—that members of an organization hold to be the true way for operating. These traditions serve as a measure, a device by which people can judge the adequacy of ideas being imposed on their work environment. The newly proposed change in direction and its implementation activities must find resonance with the established culture and established practices.

All organizations display evidence of a culture. There is an overriding organizational culture, and departments within the enterprise have their own cultures. Any time people work together for an extended period of time, a culture is formed. It is the force that guides and directs how people will interact with one another and deal with those beyond their group.

Cultural attributes discussed earlier in Chapter 4 interact in the following way to create a result: This mixture of values, norms, beliefs, symbols, and philosophies combine to produce specific feelings, a state of mind, which in turn influence how people will behave when carrying out work assignments (Fishbein and Ajzen, 1975). For example, a person can feel appreciated because the culture values teamwork and employee decision making. This cooperative atmosphere makes the individual feel good about the job and resulting work contributions. Consequently, the employee is cooperative, productive, and enthusiastic about proposed changes as well as the organization's future prospects.

Because culture has such a large impact on individual actions and how people accomplish work, there may be an overwhelming temptation to tamper with cultural attributes—values, norms, and beliefs. However, culture is created and shaped by a cascade of influences. The actions displayed are a product of many interactions. The influencing elements are contingencies that cannot be easily manipulated. So, as the leader considering how to make upgrades permanent, do not try to reshape underlying cultural attributes. Focus instead on the mechanisms that drive attribute formation and will influence changes through the expression of new attitudes and improved results. The following are means that will create a constancy of action and anchor the newly defined purpose within the organization's culture:

- Define and communicate the organization's purpose and direction. Set a future course that is consistent with the needs and expectations of customers, employees, and stakeholders.
- Develop and communicate strategies that provide a logical means for moving in the new direction. Create buy-in by approving plans that are consistent with the proposed future vision and the organization's ethical standards.
- Facilitate the creation of an infrastructure that will make it possible for people to work toward the new goals. Ensure that the methods developed for organizing and coordinating resources, communication, and labor are consistent with the espoused value system.

■ Facilitate the development of people practices that are considered fair, compassionate, and enabling. Included practices are related to hiring, employee development, promotion, discipline, and termination. Also, make sure people have the right training so that operating within revised work structures is not intimidating.

■ Ensure there is clarity in performance standards and how outcomes will be measured. Performance standards describe the boundaries for responsibility and authority. Job descriptions and work instructions are examples. When adapting the culture to a change in direction, develop processes in such a way that expectations for results are clearly stated and deemed by the workforce to be reasonable.

■ Display actions and behaviors that set an example. Above all, mirror what is being advocated for the workforce, be consistent, exemplify espoused organizational values, and place customers first. You are the role model. People at all levels will mimic and honor your example. Set a standard that others inside and outside the organization can emulate.

Interpreting the Organization's Purpose through Planning

Once the organization has developed and installed its sense of purpose, a set of actions is required that will get people moving toward the anticipated future. This is typically done by further developing long-term goals and supporting tactical objectives that can guide the enterprise in the realization of its intention. Planning translates goals and objectives into sequential steps that make achievement possible. Planning helps the leader articulate the organization's future and then orchestrate change by creating a visible road map.

The process starts by understanding the market, customer needs, and competitor capabilities. Knowledge about customers and their desires and the marketplace is primary to managing the organization's growth and ongoing survival. Merging information about customers with social, political, and financial risk factors to understand potential impact and possible hazards provides a picture of the terrain that must be navigated so the organization's purpose can be realized. The enterprise's own capabilities are studied, including human resource potential, physical plant capability, technology utilization, and supplier capacity. All this information is translated into meaningful data, forecasts, and models that executives and managers can use to analyze and evaluate prospective opportunities and threats.

Planning at its core is a process for interpreting the organization's purpose so executives, managers, and work groups can, through their own initiative, move the enterprise in a direction that will accommodate customers, clients, and stakeholders. Planning facilitates decision making—the process of selecting a course of action in response to acquired information and day-to-day realities. Decisions are made at many points as executives and managers mobilize resources in response to competitor actions and market demands. Planning is the first step toward purpose realization and the beginning of the Plan-Do-Study-Act cycle toward organizational learning and continual improvement.

Plans produce both short-term and long-term goals. Unfortunately, there is a trade-off between these two conditions: The short-term perspective is amplified by continual pressure to meet day-to-day objectives. Short-term tactics dominate actions; long-term approaches receive little or no attention until shortly before a project is due or a specific deadline. People feel decisions can be delayed because current activity will somehow narrow future options—that choices will be better down the road when more data are available. Long-term possibilities are distorted by the need to make this week's objectives or this quarter's numbers. So, those projects and activities that will incrementally bring about change and allow the organization to become more effective, more proficient, and more competitive are neglected and left mostly to chance.

Excessive emphasis on current numbers has the potential of choking the investment of time and resources that may be necessary for achieving growth several years in the future. The focus on short-term needs must be balanced by a collection of measures that have equal importance and are linked to prospects that have both short-term and long-term payoffs.

Plan deployment requires executives and managers to monitor environmental factors regularly so that adjustments can be made to ensure organizational success. For this to happen, there must be an ongoing process that measures, collects, and analyzes data so timely decisions can be made and events managed rather than reacted to as surprises. A critical action in achieving desired results includes, as part of the planning process, the development of performance measures. If done correctly, the assessment schemes chosen can serve long-term needs by allowing individuals to evaluate and manage their own work. An organization's performance measurements should focus on inputs, key process elements, and results. The combination should create a balanced scorecard for aligning activities and ensuring value for customers and stakeholders. When using a balanced scorecard approach, both financial and nonfinancial measures assume equal importance and are part of a system for monitoring that engages all organizational levels. Planning is the beginning of focused action that will move the organization from its current less-desirable condition to one of sustained improvement. The following tasks are accomplished through planning:

- Planning provides the means for interpreting and deploying the organization's purpose—vision, mission, and values.
- Planning provides the basis for decision making by establishing goals, objectives, and measures, and the means for achieving them.
- Planning links controlling with doing, then facilitates the process of corrective action and continual improvement.

Appreciating That the Job at Hand Has Just Begun

Creating and then anchoring a proposed change in direction can be rather challenging even when the approach is consistent with the existing culture. Largely because people are accustomed to the rituals and routines of the organization, they have adapted their lives to system difficulties and made its process work. Now, however, the social order and prevailing realities will be changing. There is recognition that the old command—the old heroes—will be replaced by new individuals more adept at playing in the new game.

So, now that a purpose—defined by mission, vision, and value statements—has been proclaimed, effort toward a transformed operation is just beginning. Future success will require actions that support realization. Start by doing the following:

- *Selling and telling:* Begin a well-orchestrated campaign that will put forth the word and keep the new direction at the forefront in people's minds. Appeal to all constituencies and let them know why changes are needed.
- *Identifying formal and informal networks and securing their participation:* Make sure the voices of diverse work groups are heard, and that their involvement is encouraged and rewarded. Find those who are not content with the status quo, regardless of their official standing in the current hierarchy, and ensure their involvement.
- *Creating the opportunity for small but meaningful gains:* Look for and initiate projects in which people can take risks and see clear results within a short period of time. Success breeds success by showing that the new way works.
- *Empowering people to take action:* Give problem solvers and eager work groups the authority to make changes and accept responsibility for decisions related to their

actions. Harness the energy of capable and willing work groups toward goals and objectives that are consistent with the new purpose.

■ *Providing a mechanism for addressing injustices and dealing with entrenched power:* Ensure that decisions by work groups are not reversed without consultation and consent of members. Use available political clout to deal with power structures that may undercut well-made decisions affecting change activities. Link promotions and rewards to the new way of doing business. Make it clear that the old way will not work, and that buy-in or moving on is the option.

As one more word of advice, a certain amount of pushback is a fact of life when introducing an organization to new ideas. However, when abnormal resistance occurs, it could be a signal that something may have been missed, that concerns may not have been satisfactorily handled, or the need for a change in direction may not have been adequately presented and thus may have been misunderstood. If resistance does not appear to be distributed normally—for example, there is lots of immediate and hostile opposition—that is probably an indicator that something was overlooked. People may have been overwhelmed or recognize there are catastrophic risks. The proposed effort could have fatal flaws. In any case, do not move ahead insistently without understanding why the opposition is abnormal. As the leader, your power has limitations, and your cause can be overwhelmed and swamped by a determined opponent. Make sure the need and reason for the new change in direction—mission and vision—are clear and well founded, and that the opposition does not have political motives that are substantially grounded by facts.

Chapter 7

Manage the Dynamics, Interdependencies, and Interactions

Introduction

Leadership, as defined by the competencies discussed in the first chapter, is all about managing the relationships, the interactions, and the interdependences that characterize the system of profound knowledge. Although first described by W. Edwards Deming and later defined in his book *The New Economics for Industry, Government, Education* (1994), the chapters of this book seek to clarify and promote his ideas as an advantageous strategy for leading and managing in today's environment.

The four interlocking segments that comprise the system of profound knowledge cannot be separated. These elements interact with each other to create a comprehensive body of knowledge that sets a different standard for leadership. A style for managing that recognizes individual performance is largely dominated by the system in which people work, and responsibility for that system belongs to those personalities at the top or those in control—the leadership itself. Accordingly, this chapter looks at the tasks assigned to leadership, as well as management, and describes how these activities might be accomplished considering the influence and interaction of components that make up the system of profound knowledge. The topics covered are as follows:

- Plan for the future
- Create less structure and share tasks
- Delegate and coordinate
- Problem solve and make decisions
- Monitor results
- Drive out fear
- Build trust
- Final thoughts

Plan for the Future

Although the system of profound knowledge does not specifically address the issue of planning, the task of installing and applying its principles will require forethought, coordination, and control. But, getting to that place where the system's elements become a matter of routine means there has to be a systematic course of action defining how events will be rolled out and implemented. Unfortunately, serendipity and fate cannot create an environment that is willing and accepting. So, planning becomes the vehicle for getting from here (the current state) to there (the desired state). Planning is the activity that sets the PDSA cycle—Plan, Do, Study, Act—in motion and makes such a transformation possible.

However, before the process of planning can begin, a reason is needed for doing what is about to be done. Answer the question, Why are we doing this? And, the response to this query is really a personal choice based on the organization's current needs and circumstances. However, every plan is built around an idea, a strategy for making organizational operations better. So, planning needs to start with a well-defined concept and work toward implementation and a means for ensuring results meet expectations. Planning is a formalized process that describes future results and integrates these ideas into current operations using decision making. Because planning starts with an idea—a goal, a strategy—the leader who is about to embark on such an adventure needs to articulate a meaningful future. Anyone who cannot define a plausible future (that is, define to the satisfaction of others "What's in it for me?") will have difficulty developing plans that others will find compelling. Planning is not a spectator sport. It needs to involve all those who have a stake in the results.

The decision to pursue a new strategic direction requires a future disposition and a long-term commitment to customers and stakeholder communities, including the employees who helped create current realities. Since planning implies change, then the process should be managed with thoughtful consideration for the concerns of organizational personnel and other stakeholders. Here are some points to keep in mind when considering and initiating a change in direction:

- *Make strategy development everyone's job:* Involve both employees and other constituent groups in the planning process, including external stakeholders.
- *Provide information:* Keep everyone informed. Provide access to the information needed for strategy development and decision making. Make participants aware of situational factors that created the need for change. Describe plausible benefits and consequences of proposed improvements and identify the steps that will be followed during implementation.
- *Clearly describe the process:* Translate the planning process into operational terms so involved parties understand

the procedure, its steps, and requirements for action once strategic objectives become the working reality.

■ *Treat the process of implementation with consideration:* Many organizational members will identify the change in direction as an unwelcome disruption in daily activities that now provide a sense of comfort and stability. The consequential shift in routine work structures, activities, and outcomes, can become threatening when people are left to their own coping devices. Provide for training and follow-up support.

A substantial number of books and articles have been written about the topic of planning. There are individual preferences and techniques that can be used to manage the process. Although an abundance of information is readily available, trying to reach consensus on a strategic planning method may produce a variety of opinions. Therefore, the process of setting direction should begin by ensuring that all contributors are on the same page and have a common understanding about the procedure. Accordingly, the following discussion provides a simple and straightforward approach that can be used in conjunction with many planning methods.

The planning process consists of a sequenced progression of tasks that includes strategy development and strategy deployment. Strategy development starts by defining the reasons and objectives, a common understanding, for pursuing a different future, then describing current needs and capabilities so appropriate changes can be made to realize improvement. Deployment, on the other hand, lays out the steps that will be followed to integrate the newly developed strategies into daily activities so improvements become the preferred way of operating. Table 7.1 details the process.

As illustrated, the process includes both inquiry and decision making that lead to the deployment of specific objectives. These activities correspond to the first two steps of the PDSA cycle. Once accomplished, the last two steps come into play,

Table 7.1 Strategy Development and Deployment

Phase 1: Define Objectives	Phase 2: Define Current Conditions	Phase 3: Develop a Course of Action	Phase 4: Monitor and Control
1. What is our business?	1. What are our strengths and capabilities?	1. Explain objectives and the need for making improvements	1. Establish key performance indicators for system and workforce results
2. Who are our customers and stakeholders?	2. What are customer needs and expectations?	2. Communicate a unifying purpose	2. Define decision limits for indicators
3. What values and principles should guide our relationships?	3. What are our stakeholder and employee needs?	3. Identify formal and informal work groups and ensure their participation	3. Monitor key performance indicators for system and workforce results
4. Who are we?	4. What are our environmental conditions like?	4. Create a plan for action	4. Analyze results data and make adjustments to keep programs on track
5. Where do we want to be in the long term?	5. What is our financial condition like?	5. Identify the opportunity for small but meaningful gains	
6. What are several key goals for our future improvement?	6. What are potential barriers?	6. Empower people to take action	
	7. What are our options?	7. Manage resistance to improvement	
	8. What are our strategic objectives?	8. Complete the restructuring of daily activities	
		9. Sustain and improve	

ensuring that actions conform to plans. Simply put, completing the cycle provides a means of control that assesses deployment robustness and allows for adjustments. Control keeps actions on track and within desired expectations.

Planning is all about getting from one place to another. If the four elements that comprise the system of profound knowledge are to become an active reality and part of day-to-day operations, then developing a road map that others can follow is a necessary starting point. Plans provide clarity, align multiple interests, stipulate the basis for assessment, and guide revision so objectives are accomplished. Planning is a tactic for organizing and implementing an overall strategy that will move the organization toward a different future.

Create Less Structure and Share Tasks

Deming (1994) recognized the need for modification as environmental conditions changed. Here are his thoughts on the topic for setting direction and managing structure to maintain the organization's focus.

> Anything less than direction of everyone's best efforts toward achieving the whole organization's aim is a verdict toward failure to realize best overall results. Everybody loses; even the people in successful profit centers lose. Management's job is thus clear: to achieve best results for everybody; everybody wins. Time brings changes that must be managed—must be predicted so far as possible with clarity. Because growth in size and complexity will be influenced by external forces (competition, new products, and new requirements) management will be required to alter the efforts of system components. An additional responsibility of management is to change system boundaries so the aim is better

served. Change will require the redefinition of organizational components. (p. 52)

The business of doing business takes place in an organizational setting that is buffeted by complexity. Various environmental factors influence how the enterprise will sort out and structure decision-making functions. So, some discussion about the underlying dynamics might be helpful in determining how the elements of profound knowledge can be deployed and ultimately put into operation under prevailing conditions. In a fast-moving and rapidly changing business environment, the traditional tiered structure can make communication difficult. The layering of managerial and departmental configurations in a vertical pattern tends to slow information flow and, accordingly, the ability to make rapid decisions. Although this arrangement assigns responsibility and authority to establish accountability, it often discourages risk taking and point-of-contact determinations that are frequently needed in changing or dynamic environments.

Organizations normally conduct their business within the bounds of several common environments. That is, the ability to do business is influenced by cultural norms, legal-political considerations, economic conditions, competitive forces, and the educational or skill level of employees. These operating conditions can be situated along an environmental spectrum that ranges from stable to unsettled. Both influences work in opposition to create specific pressures that can affect operational efficiencies. Typically, however, little forethought is given to the existing organizational arrangement and why practices are as they are. The current way of doing business most likely grew out of necessity and in response to competing environmental forces. Although shaped by natural selection and now historically comfortable, the present way of functioning may not be truly effective under prevailing conditions. A recent example of this dilemma is the U.S. automotive industry. The industry as a whole, hierarchically structured with centralized decision making, has not been able to compete against a host of foreign firms that developed more decentralized and less-hierarchical structures.

The lesson that emerges is that structure should match the needs and circumstances imposed by environmental conditions. With that end in mind, Burns and Stalker (1961) studied a variety of companies to see if particular patterns existed and which might be more successful. They concluded organizations operated along a continuum that ranged from mechanistic (highly structured) to organic (less structured) and found organic organizations were more flexible and adaptable under a wide range of conditions. Table 7.2 contrasts these two ends of the scale. This same idea was later supported by Lawrence and Lorsch (1967) when their research examined 10 companies and organizational structures in comparison to the external environment.

When considering and selecting an organizational configuration, leadership must also understand the relationship between influential factors like goals, external environment, organizational size, and technology use. These factors to a large extent dictate where on the mechanistic–organic spectrum an enterprise will fit.

Table 7.2   Comparison between Organizational Operating Configurations

Managerial Practices	Mechanistic Structure	Organic Structure
Hierarchal arrangement	Centralized	Decentralized
Managerial authority	Broad	Minimal
Coordination and control	Formal and impersonal	Informal and personal
Rules and procedures	Extensive and wide ranging	Few and only when necessary
Division of labor	Clear and well defined	Unclear and ambiguous

Goals: Goals define the organization's outlook in relationship to investors, customers, employees, and other stakeholders, while it operates in an environment shaped by rules and competitive pressures. Over time, through either trial and error or considered determination, the organization has developed a set of survival strategies and tactics. To a large extent, these strategies deal with growth rate and market share. Some businesses emphasize efficiency and stability; others stress adaptability and flexibility as the answer to survival. In addition, some organizations look to market dominance as a way to endure, and others look to innovation and growth. Goals set direction and explain the underlying organizational philosophy. The questions Who are we? and Where do we want to be? are answered.

Environment: Environment deals with conditions the organization must operate under and is influenced by the power of competitors, the strength of regulations, and the performance of economic forces. Environments tend to range from being stable to changeable to turbulent. These factors combine to create opportunities and threats. Large powerful organizations often push for stability where efficiencies can be exploited and profits maximized because of size. On the other hand, smaller and more nimble organizations often find opportunity in changing or turbulent circumstances that favor innovation and flexibility. Because environmental circumstances are continually in flux and require constant study, conditions that are static today can become dynamic tomorrow; thus, there is a need to be highly adaptive.

Size: Size, of course, considers the number of resources utilized and controlled in the creation of products or services. Enterprises tend to be categorized as large, medium, or small. Large organizations are generally rich in several areas and reliant on few outside sources. Conversely, small organizations are rich in one or a few areas and reliant on many outside sources.

Technology: Technology refers to the means for generating products and services. Concerns are the facilities, equipment, and methods used, including capital and human resources. Traditionally, production was viewed as batch- or process-oriented. Units of output moved from start to finish in small or large batches as opposed to a continuous flow. Hard goods like cell phones tend to be batch-oriented in contrast to chemicals like fuels or paint, which tend to flow continuously. Today, there are one-piece flow techniques that reduce some of the problems associated with batch manufacturing. Technology can also be viewed as innovative and state of the art or traditional and unfashionable. Most organizations operate using a combination of technologies. However, the demand for high levels of productivity and quality favor the use of more current technologies. Staying up to date tends to favor technology and place a demand on capital resources but reduce the need for human resources. In contrast, low-wage producers depend more on labor and underuse the latest in technology.

Recent history, at least in the United States, Western Europe, and parts of Asia, appears to favor organizational structures that that are less rigid, support innovative technology, and are capable of repeatable and predictable levels of quality and service. Successful organizations in this environment tend to cluster more toward the organic end of the scale. However, in mature industries with subdued competition—like utilities, natural gas, oil, coal, and heavy manufacturing—the structure tends to be more mechanistic. In either case, hybrid designs can combine elements from each configuration.

The Ford Motor Company, as an example, is an organization that was very mechanistic, very traditional; however, management recognized this arrangement was simply not agile enough to compete with Asian automobile manufacturers. Over a period of several years, the company became an amalgam, having a mechanistic core within an organic shell. Basic operations, although consolidated and leaner, remained traditional in structure; those business areas that deal with external matters, such as marketing, purchasing, customer affairs, and to some extent new product development, became organic in configuration. Microsoft, on the other hand, grew in fame and stature by being an organic organization, but as it matured, the arrangement shifted toward an organic core protected by a mechanistic shell. Technically sophisticated and innovative product development areas are separated from functional aspects such as finance, production, marketing, and human resources, which now have a very traditional structure.

Since most organizational arrangements tend to be shaped through the strength and personality of previous and current leaders in response to conditions, it is important to recognize and consider that the existing structure may not be a sufficient arrangement for operating in the established environment. In a world where economic conditions are far from stable, where markets favor flexibility, and where customers expect high levels of quality and service, the organizational design should promote conditions that balance the need for standardization against the ability to improve continually. This of course raises the question of whether to perform a complete makeover or to improve the current operation. In each case, people's routines and customary way for operating will be upset. Structural change also means social change, which, if not handled with consideration and care, will bring resistance and the potential for pushback. What follows are some factors to consider when approaching a redesign in organizational configuration:

■ Start by asking these questions: How does the current process or method help us serve our customers? Can it be done more effectively and efficiently some other way?
■ Involve a broad range of stakeholders when making the decision.

- Remember that issues will not be resolved until changes or improvements are successfully implemented.
- Stakeholder values and self-image, not just operating structures, will be impacted by change and implementation activities.
- Stakeholder needs and feelings must be considered and accommodated to make alterations permanent, because structural change is contingent on individual change.
- Individual change is adaptive, multistep, and dependent on people's ability to make coping adjustments.
- Actions that are planned and sequenced to assist coping have greater acceptance and a better chance of permanent adoption.

Improvement, no matter how insignificant, can have consequences. Good ideas, although meant to be implemented, are often put into practice without much planning or forethought, simply as a matter of routine. So, care should be taken before resolutely moving ahead. Individuals seldom resist technical change but act in response to social change. Those alterations that can have an impact on relationships, group order, and well-being are often a point of contention. People do not resist change; they resist the pain and threats that come from it (Scholtes, 1998). The workforce will need to understand "why" or feel they have a stake in the outcome. Open communication and direct involvement by those affected will go a long way toward reducing resistance.

Individuals are most effective and efficient when there is the right mix of freedom and direction—the freedom to make decisions without being micromanaged or second guessed, along with sufficient direction so goals, safety, and the rights of others are not set aside in the struggle to achieve overall results. Although management's job is characteristically focused on shareholder wealth, it cannot single-handedly guarantee results without consideration for and the direct involvement of the workforce or other stakeholders and customers. And, like those at the organization's top, these individuals cherish the ability to exercise control over the forces that shape their lives, particularly their work lives. Being too mechanistic and too directive tends to suppress the ingenuity and creativity that is needed in a rapidly changing world.

Structure is the organizational arrangement that enables actions toward the achievement of goals. If the design is at odds with environmental and human resource considerations, then getting the work done with ease will be difficult. The organization as a matter of course will function, but achievement of its goals may be plagued by bickering and inconsistent outcomes. An organizational structure that encourages teamwork, point-of-contact decision making, and continued learning will be most successful in today's environment. That means operating more like a startup, more organically with a relatively flat structure that is linked by open and instantaneous communication so people can make informed decisions. The focus should be on customers and how to better serve their needs. This is a rallying point that the workforce will readily recognize as the real means to organizational wealth. Without a steady stream of satisfied and repeat customers, there is no business. People understand this simple truth and will do their best to make it happen. So, do not overstructure, do not overregulate, and do not overmanage. Treat the workforce just like you want the political establishment to treat your enterprise. The same reasoning applies whether you are at the top or on the front lines trying to make an honest living.

John Kotter, in his book *Leading Change* (1996), lists the following attributes as the foundation of a 21st-century organization:

Structure
- Nonbureaucratic, with fewer rules
- Limited to fewer levels
- Organized with the expectation that management will lead and employees will manage their own areas of responsibility

- ■ Characterized by policies and procedures that produce just the right level of independence and interdependence so customer needs are served

Systems

- ■ Dependent on many information systems that provide data, especially about customers and other organizational operations
- ■ Distribute performance data on management and production systems widely
- ■ Offer training and support to managers and people at all levels

Culture

- ■ Externally oriented
- ■ Empowering
- ■ Open and candid
- ■ Quick at making decisions
- ■ More risk tolerant
- ■ Learns from its mistakes

Delegate and Coordinate

Delegation is all about the distribution and assignment of responsibility, accountability, authority, and power. It is the mechanism for dividing tasks so the overall goals of the organization can be accomplished. Delegation assumes that those at the top of the managerial pyramid have ultimate responsibility for the success or failure of operations within the enterprise. For delegation to work properly, there needs to be a descending chain of command, a line of authority that is clearly identified with jobs that are plainly defined and logically organized. Otherwise, without this basic order, there is the chance that gaps or overlaps might develop, leaving some tasks underperformed and others performed by competing interest groups with different objectives in mind. So, the critical starting point is clarity about structure and how work will be organized.

When working properly, delegation has several advantages. First, it speeds decision making by allowing those with the clearest view of issues the opportunity to resolve problems and implement solutions. Second, and probably more important, delegation provides leaders with the chance to focus on future requirements that will create new efficiencies and new opportunities for growth. But, in spite of these advantages, managers are often reluctant to share power—to delegate responsibility and authority. This happens frequently because people in positions of influence underestimate the capabilities of subordinate work groups, are not good at planning and organizing so work can be delegated, or simply fear the potential loss of power when others perform well. The basic requisite in effective delegation is the willingness to share power. However, the need to be in control—to have power—is often a point of contention when it comes to delegation.

Power is the ability to exert influence. To have power is the capacity to direct someone else's behavior, to get work done in a manner that is advantageous for the individual or group with authority. In an organizational setting, legitimacy—the right to exercise power—is usually based on structure or an individual's and possibly a group's position in that structure. However, power can come from other sources, both organizational and individual. Foremost is the ability of an individual or operating unit to cope with uncertainty and resolve critical problems that affect others in the organization. By virtue of expertise, special knowledge, or ability, these individuals are able to get required tasks and more done when others cannot. The result is respect and admiration that becomes the basis for influence and power.

In either case, legitimate power can have consequences. Because power is typically used to enhance survival through the control of resources, through the placement of loyalists in key positions, and through the creation of favorable policies or strategies, the organization can become more functional, but just as regularly becomes more dysfunctional. Such influence may in time extend power well beyond the realm of normal control, creating difficulties in other organizational work areas or, in some cases, shifting focus and strategic goals to narrow, self-serving purposes. This fact that power tends to evolve around critical issues, activities, and scarce resources makes the control of such contingencies a prime consideration when developing organizational structures and assigning tasks. The means and access to supporting resources must be clearly understood when assigning responsibility.

In the ideal situation, of course, power is shared, and organizational units have an equal opportunity to acquire resources and work jointly on critical issues so the organization's work is done in the best interests of customers and stakeholders. Power, in this case, is communal because no single unit or individual controls all the opportunities or critical activities. However, as environmental realities change, organizational contingencies often change, thus providing an opening to expand influence and enlarge boundaries. Such situational prospects and corresponding tactical maneuvers are a fact of organizational life, which can have several implications for the management of power. The first approach would be the assurance of equal access to information so individual unit leaders are aware of environmental vagaries and realities. This means paying more attention to factors that may become critical issues as organizational conditions change. Second, jointly as a management team, consider and deal with contingencies as problems arise. Involve those with relevant experience and expertise regardless of their place in the organization. Create an environment of mutual dependency and trust so people feel they can make mistakes, ask for help, obtain assistance, and recover without being disadvantaged. Third, develop a sense of community where people feel recognized and cared about; there is not only consideration for personal needs and boundaries, but also a shared responsibility for the organization's overall well-being. And last, create and continually reinforce a clear enabling organizational purpose that people can rally around and use it as a common focal point.

So, in the end, delegation is not only about the distribution of tasks and the requisite responsibility that accompanies it, but also about sharing power so others have the necessary authority to manage their own activities. Yet, power has the potential to corrupt, to distort structural arrangements toward the advantage of a few and the disadvantage of others, putting someone else's ability to operate effectively in jeopardy. Coordination becomes a mechanism that a leader can use to link actions of individuals and work units into a constructive and consistent pattern of collaboration. Available are a mixture of tools that can be used to gain the necessary cooperation so everyone is pursuing the same goals.

> *Create and communicate a common set of values:* These are principles that the organization considers the right way of accomplishing work. Values are standards for individual conduct during interactions with others inside and outside the organization. Values are the ethical and moral underpinning for behavior. These are usually built through selection, training, application, and reinforcement.
>
> *Routinely review goals and plans and update as contingencies change:* Develop an open process for creating and reviewing goals and accompanying plans. Track progress and make revisions as organizational and environmental conditions change. Make the information used in decision making available throughout the organization. Let everyone know where the organization is heading and the reasons for pursuing specific goals.
>
> *Create a user-friendly management information system:* This should be the means by which administrative data are transmitted to all levels in the organization for decision making. Management information systems typically contain record-keeping data related to finance, marketing, production, and other operations so figures are available

for planning, coordination, control, and the timing of critical efforts.

Ensure lateral communication is open and accurate: This is information that flows across the chain of command and is typically built on personal relationships. Such communication can be enhanced by creating boundary-spanning roles using committees, task forces, and cross-functional teams. In addition, monitor the grapevine and challenge inaccurate information with facts that are introduced back into the system using informal operatives. Create an official news source or online bulletin board that maintains a neutral tone, but also allow and encourage worker-run bulletin boards and newsletters that are open, yet represent contrasting viewpoints.

Use written rules, policies, and procedures: These include employing operating standards, such as an International Organization for Standardization (ISO) compliant quality system, or following criteria that support the Baldrige National Quality Program. Create rules and procedures designed to handle routine events so work groups and managers can take action without unnecessary deliberation and act in a timely fashion. When developing best practices or standard ways for operating, make sure documentation is simple yet sufficient enough to create uniformity without repressing creativity and ingenuity. Overregulation is not the objective, but freedom to operate in a consistent manner is; a delicate balance that may take some testing using trial-and-error refinements.

Set the right example through behavior and actions: As the leader, do not display privileged, guarded, or contrary behavior. A mixed message is sent that cannot be easily explained away. Actions that avoid exposure to discomfort or obscure lack of sincerity set an example that can raise resistance and discourage risk taking. People will quickly recognize their vulnerability and look for defensive strategies that can prevent further participation and learning.

Do not be caught saying one thing, then doing another. Be aggressive in calling other executives and managers to task when they fail to follow the established rules, policies, and values.

The process of coordination has two characteristics: the development of practices that are relevant to harmonizing operations, including the coordination of different work units within the organization, and the creation of a system for communicating that is both vertical and horizontal, yet has minimum potential for distortion. This is usually achieved by introducing a communication capacity that is both electronic and traditional, providing for face-to-face interaction, printed messages, and online media sources, and using many different approaches, including meetings, memos, e-mails, posters, newsletters, personal contact, and electronic databases. When communication is coming from many directions, it is not likely to be ignored or misunderstood. Organizations that are structured to encourage power sharing—independent problem solving, and decision making—need robust and capable communication so policies, procedures, and operational improvements become uniformly integrated into daily routines. Although open and unrestricted communication appears to be the ideal, attaining free interaction is not an easy task. Make sure information is accurate, available, and impartial when needed so it will be accepted as reliable and honest.

Problem Solve and Make Decisions

Problem solving and decision making are closely related activities that interact to produce answers—a course of action for overcoming obstacles when actual events do not yield desired results. The process of problem solving usually produces options, and decision making cuts away alternatives to find the best solution.

A leader's reputation can be enhanced or undercut based on the ability to solve problems and move the organization with certainty in an advantageous direction. Although there is a tendency to see individuals at the top of an organization as influential and able to unravel tough issues, problem solving and the ability to make good decisions should be the job of individuals at all levels. Successful organizations are those enterprises where problems are resolved as difficulties arise and at the location where the trouble first occurred. Nevertheless, the leader is going to be judged on ability to keep the organization out of harm's way and on the capacity of operational units to remain effective and efficient. This means day-to-day issues will have to be dealt with and improvements made that keep customers, clients, or constituents happy and returning. Problem solving and the associated decision making must produce results that have a lasting impact.

Unfortunately, when confronted with problems, many people rely on informal methods to find answers. These include traditions—past practices or experience—that apply the same decision making used in previous or similar situations. Conversely, this type of routine thinking is more appropriate if rules, policies, or work instructions can be used to guide actions. Too often, the search for remedies is susceptible to pressure for an answer, and there is a rush to reach conclusions. In response, individuals simply fall back on prior experience that employs seat-of-the-pants logic, which usually produces unsophisticated solutions. Problem solving and decision making become mental exercises with an issue confronted and an answer divined through mostly intuition and hunch.

Problem solving is more than the discovery of a workable solution. It is a systematic and rigorous process that keeps individuals from jumping to conclusions without first considering why events are the way they are and then evaluating causes based on the underlying facts. Long-term improvement

Table 7.3 Problem-Solving Methods

Rational Problem Solving	Six Sigma	Process Improvement
Problem Resolution		
Define the problem	Define	Define the need
Understand the current situation	Measure	Understand the current process
Analyze root causes	Analyze	Identify inefficiencies
Develop solutions		Develop improvements
Solution Implementation		
Implement solutions	Improve	Apply improvements
Evaluate results	Control	Evaluate results
Integrate into daily work		Make corrections

does not happen because individual decision makers are intuitive and perceptive thinkers, but because of careful pragmatic work by which data are gathered, causes identified, potential fixes evaluated, and improvements deliberately implemented. Both problem solving and decision making, through which outcomes continually produce meaningful results, come from rational methodologies using purposeful strategies. These frameworks are two-phase and multistep processes requiring both problem resolution and solution implementation. Rational problem solving, Six Sigma, and process improvement are examples of this dual-phase approach. Table 7.3 illustrates the dual nature and similarity of these methods.

Other sequential and rational models can be used to unravel troubling issues and improve efficiencies. The objective in all cases is to encourage discipline and force problem solvers to ask the right questions before probing for answers. In the end, though, making a good decision and finding the right response is not enough. More important and usually more difficult is actually implementing the solution that was decided on as the right course of action. Lasting improvement is really the end result of orderly thinking and a determined effort that treats both problem resolution and solution implementation as parts of a continuing process. To be effective, problem solvers must complete all steps in the problem resolution and implementation method and be aware how each step interacts and builds toward the next move to bring about change. Making an improvement permanent is as important as identifying root causes or inefficiencies. Application steps are vital to ensuring success. Finding the right answer is only a beginning.

A well-crafted solution does not guarantee that the process or system under consideration will be made whole or permanently improved. Forethought and purposeful action toward application are the antecedents to a successful conclusion. Improvements, no matter how insignificant, can have consequences. Incorporating specific actions into the realization process that accommodate stakeholder needs and empower people to take action can ensure completion with minimum upset. The goal of improvement is fixing the gap between current performance and desired performance. Likewise, the mindset of most individuals will have to undergo a transformation so new routines are accepted and ultimately become the established reality.

Although the urge to push new ideas on the process without reflection can be tempting, doing so often works to undercut the improvement effort. Modifications that plan for and manage human relation concerns with the same attention as everyday matters will have a much better chance of acceptance. People experiencing change are less likely to feel intimidated when they can understand and anticipate how alterations may have an impact on their work and ability to contribute. A considered approach is generally viewed as less daunting and more acceptable. To be successful, improvement activities should include practices that reduce resistance and anchor the proposed improvement so others are not confronted with the same problem at some point later.

The resulting dilemma, therefore, when making improvements or implementing solutions, is not the technical aspects of change but dealing with the human behavioral issues that are inevitably encountered. Table 7.4 introduces actions that can be taken to ease the transition from idea to integrated solution.

Corrective action, like problem resolution, requires a set of well-thought-out and managed steps. The difficult job of shifting attitudes is much easier when using clearly defined actions to alter the organization's traditions. Fixes are more likely to become permanent as people grapple with new and unfamiliar routines. Improvement can bring uncertainty and frustration for people experiencing it. However, when planned and managed so anxiety is accommodated, the new way of doing work can create a sense of excitement and growth. With that end in mind, the following is a model for improvement and change that bridges the gap between problem resolution and solution implementation.

> *Create Awareness:* Let people who have not been involved in the problem-solving process know what is happening, keep them informed. Use memos, bulletin board postings, e-mails, and meetings to get the word out. Explain the need to make changes and develop a theme for the improvement effort that others can understand and buy into. For example, a theme might be "Quality is our focus." In addition, make sure problem solvers, particularly at implementation, have included the right people. Incorporate informal leaders—those who are not part of the official supervisory structure but have standing and whom others look to for guidance—and involve them in the decision-making process.
>
> *Make a Plan:* Develop a set of action steps, decide on the sequence, and assign responsibility for each step to members of the work group. Do not move ahead without first giving the implementation process some thought. If

Table 7.4　Actions to Sustain Improvement and Anchor Change

Activity 1: Create Awareness	Activity 2: Make a Plan	Activity 3: Modify and Improve	Activity 4: Standardize and Sustain
1. Explain the need for improvements 2. Communicate a unifying purpose 3. Identify formal and informal work groups and ensure their participation	4. Create a plan for action 5. Create the opportunity for small but meaningful gains	6. Empower people to take action 7. Manage resistance to process improvement	8. Complete the restructuring of daily activities 9. Continue to monitor and reinforce improvements

the change or corrective action is complex, think about breaking the plan down into bite-size chunks so progress is visible and readily measurable against anticipated due dates. Let everyone know what to expect and when activities should be completed.

Modify and Improve: Empower the people who work in the process (e.g., frontline employees) to make the necessary changes. Provide direction by establishing boundaries for action and define what the expected outcome should be. Allow the intervening work group freedom to choose how work will be handled and grant latitude in corrective actions without second-guessing or micromanaging the effort. Support the work being done by making sure there are sufficient resources and that everyone is adequately trained to operate in the new environment. In addition, look for and manage resistance to improvement. If there is sizable pushback, it may be a sign that something was missed or concerns were not adequately handled. Do not move ahead without finding out why people are unhappy.

Standardize and Sustain: Complete the restructuring of daily activities. Finish shifting organizational structures and work methods, including communication networks, so the new way becomes fully operational. Document the new process by upgrading policies, procedures, and work instructions. Develop methods for monitoring and measuring the process so ongoing effectiveness can be assessed. If outputs or behaviors fall below anticipated expectations, then initiate problem solving. Last, acknowledge and celebrate the hard work and accomplishment of all involved.

Although proceeding carefully and methodically encourages the acquisition of relevant information during problem solving, the day-to-day realities of risk and uncertainty can create difficulties during decision making. Instead of searching for an ideal choice, problem solvers often settle for something that only adequately serves the purpose. Confronted by the following challenges, people simply look for an easy way out:

- There is a lack of time or resources that does not allow an in-depth search for possible solutions.
- The information available on the nature of the problem is inadequate or incomplete.
- Perceptions about the available information are distorted or biased by competing influences.
- The aptitude or capability of decision makers is insufficient to resolve the issue they are being asked to resolve.

Since problem solving and decision making are often subject to limitations that can encourage superficial thinking rather than deeper consideration, decision makers should develop strategies for countering perceptive shortcomings. A first and obvious alternative would be seeking the advice of a competent expert. This alternative approach might involve someone who has specific experience or knowledge about the problem being conceded. Their well-thought-out considerations can be evaluated and, based on the information received and its interpretation, a choice made. However, remaining disciplined and systematic during the process is important. Care should be taken to avoid predestinated conclusions and make sure the problem is clearly defined and understood by the conferring expert so alternatives offered are truly relevant solutions.

A second technique for problem solving, using the advice and expertise of others, is a team approach; group members work through both problem resolution and solution implementation. Although sometimes difficult because group methods and disciplines are employed, the resulting solutions are often high quality. The diverse opinions and skills of members provide a broad base of experience for gathering and evaluating facts to produce satisfying solutions. Yet, problems can arise when the resolution selected produces challenging modifications for the participating problem solvers and associated work groups. Nevertheless, group involvement has these advantages:

- Expands the knowledge and resource base of those involved
- Increases understanding among team members
- Increases self-esteem and encourages commitment to the organization
- Promotes acceptance for jointly made decisions

Problem solving and decision making, when practiced using rigor and data-driven reflection, can produce high-quality answers that are the reality rather than the exception. This holds true not only at the top of the organization but also at all organizational levels, including shop floor operations. But, be aware that human nature, the struggle under daily pressures, and the demand for quick answers can cause decisions to be biased by perceptions, assumptions, and prejudices. By clearly defining problems, structuring activities, and using rational disciplined methods, these inconsistencies can be reduced. In the end, however, problem resolution is only as good as the ability of problem solvers to understand and define issues. Decisions that are based on faulty data and faulty judgment may produce answers that, although seemingly good enough, can compound to create bigger and recurring problems that need continual attention. Problem solving and the supporting decision-making process are at the heart of long-term survival. When delegated and assigned to all operational levels, they can make a difference between being a front-runner or just another business among many in a particular market.

Monitor Results

Once a solution has been implemented, problem solvers naturally breathe a sigh of relief and head toward the door, ready to grapple with other issues, including the humdrum of daily routine. But the job is not over. Although the ordeal of problem resolution and corrective action has been successful, some additional work is still required. Problem solvers and process stakeholders will want to ensure that performance is meeting expectations and that work groups are not reverting to old and familiar patterns of work and behavior. Therefore, introduce methods that facilitate the ongoing ability of process operators to monitor and measure the performance of improved processes.

Like problem solving itself, there is a tendency to rely on intuition, experience, or judgment when drawing conclusions about progress that is the result of problem-solving success. Frequently, the assumption seems to be that everything is fine if managers or supervisors are comfortable with current operations and work groups appear to be doing what needs to be done. However, because considerable resource and effort have gone into change and improvement, a performance measurement system should be developed—a scheme that contains essential metrics capable of evaluating ongoing system health. If done correctly, the assessment method can serve long-term needs by allowing individuals to evaluate and manage their own work. An effective approach for measuring, analyzing, and utilizing system information is based on the following steps, adapted from the work of Schultz (2011):

Identify desired results: Decide on key goals and expectations for the system or process recently changed. The reason for making improvements may point to the preferred result. What are customers and stakeholders looking for? Do they expect improved quality, less waste, reduced costs, fewer returns, or specific deadlines met? Understanding the desired result will ultimately point to a specific indicator.

For example, if the owner of a fast-food restaurant has concerns about how long customers wait in line to be served, then time in minutes would be good measurement for results. Or, here is another example: A hospital has introduced changes to control medication errors. Historically, the rate has been between 2 and 5 errors per 10,000 orders. Ideally, by introducing changes, problem solving should push the number of errors lower. The error rate becomes the measurement.

Establish indicators for results: Decide what will be measured and where measurement will take place. Will the indicators be input measurements, process measurements, or output measurements? Keep it simple; too many measurements can be overwhelming.

For example, again consider the fast-food restaurant. The time it takes to be served is a process measurement. In this case, the interval for waiting from entry to checkout at the cashier is probably the best indicator for service. In terms of medication errors in the hospital example, the number of orders for medication varies daily, and the number of errors also varies, so an appropriate measure would be errors per week divided by orders per week. This is a statistical measurement that can be recorded and tracked.

Define decision limits for indicators: Establish a standard or limit—a decision rule—so that people do not overreact to minor variations or fail to react when differences beyond specifications are significant. These limits should not be arbitrary but based on information that defines the system's typical capability.

Using the fast-food example, a maximum time in the ordering line under busy conditions was set at about 5 minutes. Being caught in line longer may mean having to wolf down lunch before going back to work. In comparison, the hospital has decided to evaluate average error rates under the new procedures against average rates for errors over the previous year.

Set up a data collection and feedback process: Develop a data collection plan by answering the questions regarding what, where, when, who, and how. Design a spreadsheet or check sheet so observations can be tallied or counted. Establish a means for analysis and decision making.

Again using the fast-food example, time data could be collected by selecting 30 patrons at random and timing each individual from arrival through departure at the cashier during a peak period. The results would then be recorded on a spreadsheet. In the hospital example, data might be collected on a spreadsheet indicating the type of error—wrong dose, wrong medication, wrong patient, wrong time, no medication, and failure to repeat a dose. A weekly statistic is calculated based on the number of orders issued.

Analyze information and take corrective action: Interpret the information by charting or plotting data. Compare results to the decision rule and decide what action should be taken, if any. Sometimes, the course of action will be obvious, but on other occasions, additional information and analysis may be necessary.

In the fast-food example, the service time data were placed in a histogram, with the information organized in intervals of progressively longer time, and a judgment was made about throughput time. Some customers made it in fewer than 5 minutes, others took longer than 20 minutes, but 70 percent were caught in waiting lines for between 10 and 20 minutes. Yes, according to the decision rule, there appears to be a problem. Fixing the problem, however, requires further study or experimentation. Is the problem related to having enough food prepared, or would assistance with filling orders at peak times work better? In the other example, medication errors are plotted weekly on a run chart that has the average line for previous errors indicated. If the new program is working, successive points plotted should show a trending decline that eventually settles below the previous average. If not, then the program needs to be reevaluated.

Before beginning data collection, make sure the reasons for gathering such information are clear. As discussed in the chapter on variation, the following needs repeating: Take the time to plan for data collection and analysis. Collect only what is important for understanding process issues or problem solving. There is a tendency to measure too many variables or subjective attributes that do not add clarity. When developing performance measures, look for indicators that assess proximity to standards, uniformity and stability of processes, customer satisfaction, and employee effectiveness. There should be a mixture of indicators. Include only key process characteristics and outcomes that have a clear link to project objectives and customer satisfaction. Do not focus exclusively on financial dimensions; instead, focus on those factors that will create long-term value. Such indicators might include measurements such as perfect orders shipped, on-time delivery, inventory levels, capacity utilization, lost work due to safety issues, customer delight, employee satisfaction, and employee training completed.

An organization's performance measurements should focus on inputs, key process elements, and results. The combination should create a balance of measurements for aligning activities and ensuring value. A performance measurement may be almost anything, but to have meaning and relevance, it must be supported by methods that make the information understandable. This, in turn, provides for communication that others can trust. It also produces information for decision making that others feel is likely to produce a dependable result. Performance measurements are used to assess current conditions against desired conditions. The resulting data have value that ought to be shared. Feedback, however, must do more than merely provide information that checks up on the workforce. Data effectiveness can be lost when measurement results become a disciplinary device. People will then have difficulty linking actions with results and view future information from measurement with skepticism.

System failures are seldom the direct result of individual failure. Other difficulties associated with process operations such as machinery, equipment, methods, or materials often contribute to breakdowns. Using data to make people the sole source of a problem will not determine root causes. Real solutions are found when examination of the system considers all contributing factors. Data gathering and analysis achieve legitimacy when multiple aspects are measured and evaluated. Feedback will then provide for learning. It will not create fear but will help individuals become more effective and efficient at their jobs. When monitoring operational performance, worry over reprimand is reduced if measurement and analysis are turned over to a work group for deployment. The information gathered then becomes a valuable tool and a catalyst for continued improvement. It provides information that will keep the system capable and on course. Allowing people to use the results of data analysis for their own benefit reduces the potential for resistance and helps lock in improvements.

Drive Out Fear

Workers, like businesses and their investors, prefer an environment in which risks and unknowns are kept to a minimum. People, to a large extent, would rather focus their time and energy on the business of doing business—achieving the goals and objectives of the enterprise for which they work. Unfortunately, organizational structures and behaviors often create conditions that keep the workforce from doing its best. Far too often, time is spent controlling the social forces that determine relationships, decision making, and access to resources. A prevailing sense of vigilance, of having to be on one's toes, detracts from creativity and the ability to focus on the nitty-gritty job details that keep coworkers, stakeholders, and customers happy. This underlying feeling of worry that routinely afflicts the workplace led Deming (1986) to include the following axiom as one of his 14 points to management: "Drive out fear."

Fear is the uneasy feeling of impending consequences that encourages both workers and managers to engage in defensive postures and self-protective behaviors. Such actions try to avoid exposure and the resulting discomfort that comes from negative experiences often initiated by a clash over roles: a sequence of conduct based on mistrust by which management assumes the position of parent and diminishes workers to the role of a child. This characterization then sets in motion repeated actions of aggression and self-preservation on both sides. This parent-child relationship—I am the boss, and you are not—lets management intervene with employees in ways that, under most conditions, would be deemed inappropriate for adults in a society that prizes self-determination and risk taking.

Unfortunately, management, by virtue of its position in the organizational structure and under pressure to realize outcomes, often takes a paternalistic stance as a way to ensure control and achieve expeditious results. This attitude of "I know best" subordinates the workforce. Thus, it invites resentment and pushback that is followed by more aggressive and stricter supervision, which in turn reinforces negative perceptions on both sides. The assumptions and self-protective behaviors that each group displays are described as follows (adapted from Ryan and Oestreich, 1991):

Management assumptions about employees:
- "Most of these folks don't understand the business pressures and the budgetary realities I'm under."
- "They have a hard time grasping the big picture."
- "They don't like to accept responsibility."
- "They do just enough to earn a paycheck and at times don't even do what is required."

- "They often ignore polices and stretch the rules."
- "They require well-defined limits, structured work procedures, and constant supervision."
- "There is too much concern over money, benefits, and individual rights."

Employee self-protective behaviors as a response:
- Do not speak up when problems or mistakes are uncovered.
- Restrict the flow of information upward and laterally.
- Blame management or circumstances for problems.
- Do not participate in meetings or forums where open discussion is encouraged.
- Look for opportunities to expose management's shortcomings or allow managers to make mistakes in front of others.
- Speak unfavorably about a manager or make fun of particular behaviors.
- Complain to customers, suppliers, and competition about management's failures or shortcomings.
- Openly challenge decisions.
- Ignore suggestions, directions, or orders.
- File grievances, complaints, or lawsuits.

Employee assumptions about management:
- "These people are more interested in political correctness than doing the right thing."
- "They have an elitist attitude and are obsessed with personal power and control."
- "They are preoccupied with secrecy and will do whatever it takes to protect their own careers."
- "They continually take credit for other people's ideas and purposely discount ideas that are not their own."
- "They certainly have their favorites and go out of their way to protect them."
- "They are threatened by people who might be more competent than they are."

- "They are continually trying to deny people's rights to get more work out of them."
- "They will retaliate in sinister and unscrupulous ways."
- "They think they are better than the rest of us."

Management self-protective behaviors as a response:
- Micromanage the work under their control.
- Develop more restrictive work rules.
- Institute tighter performance standards.
- Give emphasis to the formal chain of command.
- Become overly critical of mistakes.
- Emphasize formal policies, procedures, and work rules.
- Take disciplinary actions against those who appear to be ringleaders.
- Limit and control the flow of information in and out of the department.
- Reassign and transfer people who seem difficult or appear to be causing problems.
- Restrict and limit the ability of employees to communicate among each other or participate in decision making.

This cycle of suspicion is often endemic and is assumed to be the normal way for operating in many enterprises. It has at its roots classical management theory that is built on multiple levels of responsibility and authority: This is a tiered hierarchy of superiors and subordinates described by boxes and lines on an organizational chart that positions everyone from the chief executive to the lowest-level worker and an arrangement that reinforces assumptions about perceived differences and encourages polarized points of view that can lead to fear and insurgent behaviors. Unfortunately, the posturing and defensive routines set in motion a group dynamic—each side becomes committed to its own needs and norms while organizational goals become secondary—thus reducing collaboration as well as overall organizational effectiveness.

The existence of an organizational hierarchy can create competition for limited resources and individual work unit recognition. This in turn often produces a leadership dilemma that is twofold: first, how to make work groups effective at fulfilling organizational goals along with satisfying the desires of individual members; and second, how to create conditions that will facilitate work-related activity and increase organizational productivity without setting in motion destructive intergroup conflicts. Because the potential for adversarial relationships is high, goals should be focused on encouraging and sustaining collaborative associations. Start by introducing work arrangements and structures for which task independence is required to complete a job, and many activities must be harmonized to meet overall production requirements. The following is an adaptation of Schein's (1980) thinking and presents preemptive methods for encouraging work group cooperation:

Create a compelling external focus: Find and focus on common opponents. This has been a tactic employed by politicians and leaders for most of history. Look for ways of harnessing work group effort to help the organization compete against other companies in the same geographic area or enterprises in the organization's same business sector. Make a strong commitment to customer service. It is the customer who ultimately determines the enterprise's worthiness. Competing work groups can readily understand that satisfied customers ultimately pay their salaries.

Create and communicate a meaningful organizational purpose: Locate a superordinate goal. Search for a compelling and worthwhile meaning for the organization's existence. Define the enterprise's central purpose. Rally people around a theme that lets everyone know why the organization exists, what it does, and where it intends to be in the future. In addition, create a brand-new task, product line, or organizational structure that requires cooperation among previously competing groups. Give people a

meaningful reason for their work and a common determined effort.

Create an emphasis on total organizational effectiveness: Help
people understand how to function as a team. This is a
tactic that characterizes a great coach as well as a compelling leader. Provide training in teamwork, problem solving,
and conflict management. Emphasize systems thinking in
working relationships. Stress the concept: "We are all in
this together." Do not let one department or work group
optimize its operations to the disadvantage of others.
Organizational units cannot function successfully without
participating in a series of dependent interactions that are
the result of teamwork. Measure and reward combined and
total effort rather than individual or departmental success.

*Create structures that facilitate frequent interaction and high
levels of communication:* Keep a short distance between
the top and bottom levels of the enterprise. This characteristic has been the hallmark of Silicon Valley companies.
The Catholic Church for centuries has managed its affairs
with only four levels of authority. Flatness facilitates direct
communication and is a widely held concept, but is not
the only way to encourage interaction and exchange.
Create more opportunities for group problem solving and
participation in companywide decision making. Use a
team approach to develop new products. Rotate people
between departments, work assignments, and leadership
positions. Organize around lateral processes with specific
opportunities to develop ideas together. Employ a communication system that is multifaceted, user friendly, current, and comprehensive and informs everyone.

Create a culture that shows genuine caring for people: Set
the right example by treating others as trustworthy individuals with skills and abilities that contribute to the
organization's well-being. This attitude lets others know
what behavior is acceptable. People who are treated with
respect, are acknowledged and noticed, are invited to

participate, and then are listened to are more likely to act similarly in return. Develop a sense of community where people are valued, cared for, and not treated as ordinary assets. Provide opportunities to learn and grow so people can improve their work skills and develop lifelong learning that will afford opportunities beyond the job.

Fear and its antecedent, intimidation, are pervasive behaviors of organizational life. Almost daily, there are news articles about businesses, colleges, religious institutions, and governmental agencies that have betrayed the public trust by acting unscrupulously or illegally. The underlying causes for these failures are often disregarded and then encouraged because knowledgeable individuals, as the result of fear, failed to act. People were afraid of being demoted, replaced, transferred, or embarrassed. Normal, honest, and usually concerned individuals were in fear for their jobs, livelihood, or reputations because someone in a position of power made it painfully clear that speaking out would be a dangerous thing to do. In small ways, the shadowy duo of intimidation and fear play out repeatedly in many organizational settings. Quality is compromised because shipping dates must be met. Costly failures occur because maintenance is delayed. The budget is strained, and the result is downtime, lost production, or sometimes injury. Altered figures and compromised accounts, all in an effort to avoid reprimand, paint a rosy picture that leads to faulty decision making and a loss of investor confidence. These are only a few examples of how corrosive and destructive worry can be. Fear destroys trust and the ultimate ability of an organization or institution to function coherently over time.

Build Trust

Trust is a social contract that can make the difference between a highly functional organization and one that is barely functional. When people trust one another, they can anticipate how others will respond. Life becomes more predictable if less energy is devoted to defensive routines. On the other hand, when there is a relatively high level of distrust, actions and behaviors become guarded. Organizational life becomes garrisoned; work groups hunker down behind department walls and do their best to maximize individual conditions, regardless of other organizational consequences. Cooperation and optimization are ignored in a competitive race for survival.

Individuals in high places are often viewed with a certain level of skepticism and distrust because their climb often required compromise accompanied by shrewd, measured, and grasping behavior. This type of ambition often makes superiors and peers uneasy, but lower-level individuals can become extremely anxious. People recognize their vulnerability in this situation because the social construct that allows trust to build has no written or fast rules. Predictability and exposed vulnerabilities are at the convenience of the person in authority—the prevailing top dog. So, anyone who wants to be trusted by associates and subordinates must be viewed as trustworthy. This is a status that is attainable through repeated actions that demonstrate consistent behavior: a willingness not only to withhold judgment and reciprocity but also to expose personal vulnerabilities and exchange that openness for working conditions that are mutually beneficial.

True leadership requires an adaptive mindset, which displays characteristics that are uncompromising in terms of trustworthiness. People are willing to follow a trustworthy leader because they agree with the declared purpose and feel they will not be betrayed—that their investment of time, energy, emotion, and sometimes money will take them to a better place without being disappointed. Leadership is about building and keeping trust. Trust is the realization that a person as a member of a group will be treated fairly, with respect, and will have the opportunity to make a contribution that in part was their decision. Trust allows people to subordinate a portion of their individuality for the benefit of the larger community. Trust builds over time because repeated experiences have been positive and fulfilling. But, trust can be shattered in a single negative instant if well-being, imagined expectations, and hope are sacrificed for another person's ambiguous and selfish not-agreed-to purpose.

When experience demonstrates that the relationship between leader and follower cannot be trusted, rebuilding confidence can take considerable time. Trust is built by bringing together and visibly demonstrating two actions: respect (the conviction that people are capable and competent individuals able to do what needs to be done with skill) and selflessness (the belief that people are able to act in the best interests of others as well as for themselves even in challenging circumstances). When people feel they have been treated unfairly, deceived, and disrespected, they will look for an opportunity to balance the perceived injustice. Acting in an untrustworthy manner will create grousing skeptics and disheartened antagonists who in time will sink the ambitions of those who deceived them. The leader's cause will be battered by an undertow as followers try to attain their unfulfilled goals. Generally, those who have been treated responsibly and have been trusted can be rallied to a cause and will remain committed when the following happen:

- Opinions are respected and listened to. Inputs or ideas are considered and not discarded without a fair hearing or evaluation.
- People are treated honestly. There are no hidden agendas or self-serving plans that place a particular individual or work group at a disadvantage.
- Individual uniqueness is acknowledged and recognized. A coworker's situation or ability to adapt to proposed changes is considered and accommodated.
- Promises, implied or explicit, are kept. Saying one thing and doing another at the organization's convenience will only produce resistance to the improvement effort.

A leader who has lost the trust of followers but maintains position by advantage based on rank is really not a leader—just a figurehead who is presiding by default. In these situations, often driven by fear and the need to work and survive, people will follow but do only what is required and probably less. The result is an organization that is underperforming, displays dysfunctional behaviors, and is managed through paternalistic relationships that are built on self-importance and domination. The organization functions, work is done, but people cannot wait until leadership, like supermarket produce, reaches the end of its shelf life. Unfortunately, the exit often takes some devastating blow that diminishes the enterprise and alerts the board of directors that something is terribly wrong. The lesson in this case is that trusted leaders have willing followers, are much more than overseers, and with the help of others, create organizations that are energetic workplaces where learning and growth happens. True leaders have not only influence and standing but also know-how to build trust and anchor their leadership in the lessons of profound knowledge.

Final Thoughts

Leadership as discussed in this book is much more than the possession of characteristics like charisma or tough-mindedness. It is about governance and making things happen, a tough, often isolating, job that is recognized and honored through performance, usually well after the deed was accomplished. Real leadership is about understanding: knowing how to read circumstance and then consciously appreciating the consequence of actions. An effective leader recognizes that there are risks involved and then is able to set a reasoned course for action that others will follow.

Indeed, much in the media has been devoted to the bearing and presence of leaders. Popular wisdom often promotes style and flare as a desired virtue. However, many who demonstrate these characteristics share the same self-deceiving personality traits: hubris and excessive ambition. In the end, individuals of this nature who possess remarkable powers of charm and influence usually suffer catastrophic downfalls, with devastating consequences for followers and detractors alike. This is historically true and recently true as exemplified by the current Great Recession and the long ago Great Depression. Imposing individuals, during these events, were hailed as "great people" of the time, saviors of the economy or champions of business and politics. Yet, many months and years later, large populations are still living with the devastating results of the leader's inability to recognize that actions without understanding have consequences.

In recent years, leadership focus has shifted from broadbase measurements for which innovation and excellence were indicators of executive skill to short-term financial results. The driving force has become quarterly and semiannual figures lacking equal or balancing pressure from measurements that support long-term growth and strategic renewal. Shareholders, fund managers, and boards of directors have made it painfully clear that compensation and job security are based on short-term goals that ensure investor wealth. This is an incentive system that ultimately undermines durable prospects and places an enterprise's long-term survival at risk, usually revealed by the loss of customers, shareholder equity, and rank-and-file employment.

The ideas and principles discussed in this book have tried to restore a sense of balance where concern for other stakeholders and long-term performance are considered an important part of leadership character. With a similar viewpoint in mind, the *Harvard Business Review* has tried to challenge management's typical 90- to 180-day outlook by introducing new metrics for assessing best-performing executives. In its January–February 2010 issue, a new scorecard was introduced that considered an executive's entire tenure in office. The issue examined which chief executive officers and their companies were able to do well not only financially but also in terms of corporate social performance. Jeff Bezos, number two on the 2013 scorecard, reflected this wider focus when he remarked as follows (Hansen, Ibarra, and Peyer, 2013):

> When things get complicated, we simplify them by asking, "What's best for our customer?" We believe that if we do that, things will work out in the long term. We can never prove that. In fact, sometimes we do electricity studies, and the answer is that we should raise prices. But we don't because we believe that by keeping prices low, we can earn trust with customers, and this will maximize free cash flow over the long-term. (p. 82)

Effective leaders view the job of leadership as a responsibility, not as a platform for praise and limitless privilege, not as a place to show others how smart, driven, and deserving they are, but as an assignment to create collective good where outcomes are balanced against the potential for harm. When problems arise, real leaders do not place blame but instead find a plausible solution so the greater population is served, not merely a fortunate few. Because effective leaders understand the magnitude of their responsibility, they are less likely to act unilaterally and tend to surround themselves with equally competent and capable advisers who are not isolated from the population and stakeholder groups they serve. These individuals recognize they are ultimately accountable for their actions.

Effective leaders are multidimensional. As the heads of enterprise—whether business, political, or educational—they understand that actions have consequences, that actions are not isolated, but also that actions have an impact on the larger system where events take place. Therefore, the leader appreciates the relationship between component parts and balances actions toward the common good. The effective leader knows that educated and well-trained people are more capable, able to make decisions, able to improve the work process, and able to better contribute to the enterprise's overall well-being. The effective leader recognizes why people behave as they do and is able to create an environment where individual differences and skills are used to optimize the enterprise's capabilities for everyone's benefit. The effective leader grasps that two data points do not predict a trend, and that system contingencies vary over time—sometimes positive and sometimes negative—and the resulting information can be used to provide guidance about what is normal and what is not normal. Decisions and actions are based on the discovery and evidence that data bring, which are balanced against long-term objectives and consequences.

Last, and probably most important, effective leaders are trusted. Trust is the belief that those at the top will "walk the talk" and do what they say. As individuals, leaders may not be 100 percent likable, but their actions and examples have been constant over time. The values and expectations of the enterprise and its stakeholders have not been thrown over for questionable or self-serving gains. Effective leaders are viewed by followers as honest because they have demonstrated integrity through managerial decisions that bring pride and joy to work.

The following are two, somewhat contrasting, views of leadership. The first is from W. Edwards Deming and the second from Warren Bennis. Both quotations were found in the book *Empowered Business Resources* (Shelton, 1990).

> The basic cause of sickness in American industry is failure at the top to manage. ... The causes usually cited for failure are costs: startup costs, overrun costs, excess inventory cost, and competition—everything but the actual cause, which is pure and simple bad management. (Deming, 1990, p. 105; quoted in Shelton, 1990)

The factor that empowers the workforce and ultimately determines which organizations succeed or fail is the leadership of those organizations. When the strategies, processes, or cultures change, the key to improvement remains leadership. (Bennis, 1990, p. 207; quoted in Shelton, 1990)

Appendix

Choosing the Right Leader Questionnaire

Use the listed competencies and supporting criteria to assess your or a potential candidate's leadership capability. Take a long-term perspective; consider the total sweep of the person's career. Weigh and score responses based on the following scale:

0. No systematic approach
1. Beginning: A few work groups are applying this idea or approach.
2. Somewhat effective: Some work groups are applying this idea or approach.
3. Effective: Most work groups are applying this idea or approach.
4. Fully effective: Nearly all work groups are applying this idea or approach.
5. Advanced: The idea or approach is fully deployed and work groups are capable of acting on their own initiative.

Articulates a compelling future: The leader is able to define and communicate the organization's principal purpose.

- Defines the organization's principal purpose and balances it against current needs and future opportunities.
- Communicates the organization's purpose, values, and performance expectations throughout the organization and related communities.

Focuses on the long-term: The leader is able to create a map that focuses attention on the organization's long-term survival. Short-term objectives don't become distractions that restrict continual assessment and ongoing improvement.

- Orchestrates the gathering of information about the organization's markets, competition, and overall economic conditions, including technology use, budgetary conditions, and other potential risks.
- Employs the knowledge gained from gathered information, facilitates the development and deployment of action plans—used by managers and employee groups—to meet short-term objectives and long-term strategic goals.
- Balances the pressure for short-term gain against the organizations long-term survival.

Centers diverse efforts so the whole system benefits: The leader is able to manage the organization as a system by eliminating barriers between component parts so people can work together as a team for the common good.

- Promotes cooperation, collaboration, initiative, and innovation that are congruent with customer, organizational, and stakeholder needs.
- Advocates and supports effective communication, cooperation, and knowledge sharing across business functions, units, and work locations.

- Creates a compensation, recognition, and reward system that reinforces cooperative and collaborative behavior across all work locations to support organization-wide performance excellence.
- Ensures that recognition and reward system results accomplish what is wanted, and not what is rewarded. The concern for others—customers, constituents, or stakeholders—and the level of quality are not sacrificed for the reward incentive.

Provides for enabling structures: The leader is able to facilitate the development of an infrastructure that accommodates the diverse nature of human behavior and coordinates individual activities so actions align with both long-term goals and short-term objectives.

- Creates work processes that are designed, organized and administered so there is a clear understanding of responsibility, authority, and how jobs relate to unit objectives, organizational goals, and customer satisfaction.
- Provides access to information that is needed by individuals and work units to make decisions and perform daily job activities.
- Ensures there are resources, including tools, machinery, and equipment sufficient to carry out the organization's goals and unit objectives.
- Orchestrates recruiting and hiring practices that provide adequate personnel with ample skills to meet the organization's current operational and future demands.

Appreciates the impact of variation: The leader is able to recognize the inherent variability of organizational influences and individual activities, can distinguish what is normal and not normal, and understands the kind of action to take in response. The corresponding reply is based on data gathered over time, and not on point-to-point comparisons (e.g., this month's sales are down from last month's).

■ Adopts a balance of enterprise-wide measurements that are selected and used to effectively assess progress toward the realization of organizational goals and unit objectives.

■ Promotes practices that measure sources of organizational and work process variation so stability and instability can be assessed and appropriate action taken in response to each condition.

■ Ensures information collected for decision making is complete, current, reliable and accurate.

Facilitates individual and organizational development: The leader is able to provide for the development of individual and organizational capabilities by increasing access to information and learning so people working together can solve problems, make decisions, and contribute to the organization's or group's well-being.

■ Arranges for the appraisal of organizational skill requirements so educational and training programs are developed that address the enterprise's performance needs.

■ Facilitates the continual assessment of training and educational programs to ensure material and content are current and sufficient to meet individual and organizational needs.

■ Encourages the design of training and educational programs that support lifelong learning and an individual's ability to learn how to learn.

Arouses behaviors and actions that contribute to the common good: The leader understands human behavior, and uses positive reinforcement and intrinsic motivators to inspire actions that achieve outcomes aligned with the group's needs and organization's overall purpose.

■ Participates visibly in goal setting, planning, and process improvement activities, including the recognition of educational achievement and performance advancement.

- Articulates clearly and consistently acceptable organizational norms, values, and behaviors.
- Ensures that decisions by work groups are not reversed without member consultation and consent.
- Makes certain there is a mechanism in place for evaluating organizational inequalities, and provides the means for addressing injustices using political clout to deal with power structures that may undercut empowerment and the workforce's ability to freely engage in decision-making, goal setting, planning, and organizational improvement.

Displays personal credibility: The leader is able to establish a sense of personal credibility that sets an example by displaying personal ethics, managing emotions, and taking responsibility for the results of individual and subordinate actions.

- Evaluates senior management behavior to ensure that managers and supervisors walk the talk—do what is communicated and advocated.
- Ensures senior management assesses and anticipates public concerns that may arise from current and future organizational operations.
- Ensures senior management identifies and prioritizes environmental and community needs, and systematically addresses these issues within the resource capabilities of the organization.

Affinity Technique

The Affinity Technique approach is used to generate a large number of ideas and organize the results into groupings containing similar themes. It helps focus thinking and allows a few key thoughts to emerge naturally.

To use the Affinity Technique, do the following:

1. Distribute index cards or sticky notes and ask members to brainstorm ideas that convey a future focus for the improvement effort.
2. There should be one idea per card or sticky note. Use more than one word—five to eight seem to work best. Here are two examples: "Communication between groups is difficult." "Groups do not trust each other."
3. Post or otherwise display the resulting ideas so that they are visible to the entire group and ask members to physically sort the cards or sticky notes into related groupings.
4. Keep the conversations to a minimum—no talking if possible. Allow people to make associations that best fit their feelings. If an idea moves from one group to another and back several times, create a second card so the two groupings contain the same idea.
5. Once each member feels comfortable with the arrangements, ask the work group to create a header card for each grouping. The header card should contain a sentence that summarizes the thought or theme contained in each particular group of cards. An example might be: "Work groups need to function more effectively."
6. The summary sentence should be a consensus agreement that is specific and concise.
7. Then, by vote or nominal group technique, have the team rank the header cards. The card with the top vote is a likely candidate for a purpose statement.

Force Field Analysis

Force Field Analysis is a technique used to identify factors that work against a solution through finding counterbalancing reasons that can eliminate or reduce the negative factors.

On the left side of the worksheet, as illustrated in Table A.1, list constraints and other issues that may become barriers to achieving end results. Then, on the right side, brainstorm and list things that can be done to accommodate the barriers or work around them. Each negative should have at least one or possibly more counterbalancing positive forces.

The discussion encourages reflection on issues, their root causes, and plausible solutions. Prioritize work-arounds through consensus or voting and use the information as the basis for tactical plans that will improve the condition studied.

Table A.1 Example Force Field Analysis

Problem or goal statement: Reduce Operating Expenses	
Objectives: (1) Cut marketing expenses, (2) Cut outside services, (3) Reduce equipment failures, (4) Cut people costs	
Barriers/Negatives	*Work arounds/Positives*
1. Resistance from middle management and supervisors	1a. Specific program to increase two-way communication. 1b. Ensure participation by these groups in decision making. 1c. Ease adjustment through education and training.
2. The difficulties associated with scaling-up inside capabilities	2a. Initiate study to determine cost effectiveness of inside vs. outside. Review data processing and accounting services, marketing services, and consulting services. 2b. Improve timeliness, accuracy, and control of information in all operations.
3. Increase in maintenance and equipment costs	3a. Develop a comprehensive preventative maintenance program. 3b. Develop a comprehensive program for depreciating and replacing older equipment. 3c. Improve make or buy decision making with the possibility of eliminating some operations.
4. Push-back from labor at all levels	4a. Shop for new benefit package suppliers that have equivalent features. 4b. Hold the line on new heirs. 4c. Encourage retirement of older, more expensive employees. 4d. Improve efficiencies and labor's capability through training. 4e. Initiate a Lean enterprise program. 4f. Eliminate some operations as discussed in (3c) above.

References

Alderfer, C.P. (1972). *Existence, relatedness and growth: Human needs in an organizational setting*. New York: Free Press.

Apps, J.W. (1989, Fall). Foundations of effective teaching. *Effective teaching styles*, 43, 17–27.

Bennis, W., and Nanus, B. (1985). *Leaders: The strategies for taking charge*. New York: Harper & Row.

Burns, T., and Stalker, G.M. (1961). *The management of innovation*. London: Tavistock.

Carey, R.G. (2003). *Improving health care with control charts*. Milwaukee, WI: ASQ Quality Press.

Center for Applications of Psychological Type. (2012). The story of Isabel Briggs Myers. Retrieved from http://www.capt.org/mbti-assessment/isabel-myers.htm

Daft, R.L. (1983). *Organizational theory and design*. St. Paul, MN: West.

Deming, W.E. (1986). *Out of the crisis*. Cambridge: Massachusetts Institute of Technology.

Deming, W.E. (1994). *The new economics for industry, government, education*. Cambridge: Massachusetts Institute of Technology.

Drucker, P.F. (1954). *The practice of management*. New York: Harper & Brothers.

Fiedler, F.E., Chemers, M.M., and Mahar, L. (1976). *Improving leadership effectiveness*. New York: Wiley.

Fishbein, M., and Ajzen, I. (1975). *Beliefs, attitudes, interactions and behaviors: An introduction to theory and research*. Reading, MA: Addison-Wesley.

French, J.R.P., and Raven, B. (1962). The basis of social power. In Cartwright, D. (ed.), *Group dynamics: Research and theory*. Evanston, IL: Row Peterson, pp. 150–167.

Hackman, J.R. (1987). The design of work teams. In J.W. Lorsch (ed.), *Handbook of organizational behavior*. Englewood, NJ: Prentice Hall, pp. 84–95.

Hansen, M.T., Ibarra, H., and Peyer, U. (2013, January–February). The best performing CEOs in the world. *Harvard Business Review*, pp. 81–95.

Hanson, J.R., Silver, H.F., and Strong, R.W. (1986). *Teaching styles and strategies*. Moorestown, NJ: Hanson Silver Strong Assoc.

Heinen, J.S., and Jacobson, E. (October 1976). A model of task group development in complex organizations. *Academy of Management Review*. pp. 98–111.

Hersey, P., and Blanchard, K.H. (1982). *Management of organizational behavior*. 4th ed. Englewood Cliffs, NJ: Prentice-Hall.

Hunt, V.D. (1992). *Quality in America: How to implement a competitive quality program*. Homewood, IL: Business One Irwin.

Joiner, B.L. (1994). *Fourth generation management*. New York: McGraw-Hill.

Juran, J.M. (1954, November). Universals in management planning and controlling. *The Management Review*, pp. 748–761.

Juran, J.M. (1995). *Managerial breakthrough: The book on improving management performance*. 2nd ed. New York: McGraw-Hill.

Kaplan, R.S., and Norton, D.P. (1996). *The balanced scorecard: Translating strategy into action*. Boston: Harvard Business School Press.

Knowles, M. (1981). *The adult learner: A neglected species*. Houston, TX: Gulf.

Kohn, A. (1992). *No contest: The case against competition*. New York: Houghton Mifflin.

Kohn, A. (1993). *Punish by rewards*. New York: Houghton Mifflin.

Kotter, J.P. (1990, May–June). What leaders really do. *Harvard Business Review*, pp. 103–111.

Kotter, J.P. (1996). *Leading change*. Boston: Harvard Business School Press.

Kroeger, O., and Thuesen, J.M. (1992). *Type talk at work*. New York: Delacorte Press.

Laird, D. (1978). *Approaches to training and development*. Quezon City, Philippines: Addison-Wesley.

Lawrence, P.R., and Lorsch, J.W. (1967). *Organization and environment: Managing differentiation and integration*. Homewood, IL: Irwin.

Maslow, A.H. (1970). *Motivation and personality*, 2nd ed. New York: Harper & Row.

McClelland, D.C. (1961). *The achieving society.* Princeton, NJ: VanNostrand Reinhold.

Meier, D. (1995, December). *Accelerated learning: A key to individual and organizational success.* Symposium conducted by Madison Area Quality Improvement Network, Madison, WI.

Milgram, S. (1964). Group pressure and action against a person. *Journal of Abnormal and Social Psychology*, 69, 137–143.

Pfeffer, J. (1998). *The human equation: Building profits by putting people first.* Boston: Harvard Business School Press.

Price Waterhouse. (1996). *The paradox principles.* Chicago: Irwin.

Ryan, K.D., and Oestreich, D.K. (1991). *Driving fear out of the workplace: How to overcome the invisible barriers to quality, productivity, and innovation.* San Francisco: Jossey-Bass.

Schein, E.H. (1980). *Organizational psychology.* 3rd ed. Englewood Cliffs, NJ: Prentice-Hall.

Schermerhorn, J.R., Hunt, J.G., and Osborn, R.N. (1988). *Managing organizational behavior.* New York: Wiley.

Scholtes, P.R. (1998*). The leader's handbook.* New York: McGraw-Hill.

Schultz, J.R. (2006, April). Measuring service industry performance. *Performance Improvement*, 45, 13–17.

Schultz, J.R. (2008, May). Helping ease the transition. *Quality Progress*, pp. 53–58.

Schultz, J.R. (2011). *Making it all work: A pocket guide to sustain improvement and anchor change.* New York: Routledge.

Shelton, K. (ed.). (1990). *Empowering business resources.* Glenview, IL: Foresman.

Stoner, J.A.F., and Freeman, R.E. (1989). *Management.* 4th ed. Englewood Cliffs, NJ: Prentice-Hall.

Siu, R.G.H. (1980). *The master manager.* New York: Wiley.

Thomas, K.W. (1976). Conflict and conduct management. In Dunnett, M.D. (ed.), *Handbook of industrial and organizational behavior.* Chicago: Rand-McNally, pp. 1267–1349.

Tuckman, B. (1965). Developmental model in small groups. *Psychology Bulletin*, 63 (6), pp. 389–399.

Wheeler, D. (2003). *Making sense of data.* Knoxville, TN: SPC Press.

Index